OFFICIAL REPORT

OF THE

FORTY - FIRST

INTERNATIONAL CHRISTIAN

ENDEAVOR CONVENTION

Held at Grand

Rapids, Michigan

July 9 - 15, 1951

First Fruits Press
Wilmore, Kentucky
c2015

First Fruits Press

The Academic Open Press of Asbury Theological Seminary

204 N. Lexington Ave., Wilmore, KY 40390

859-858-2236

first.fruits@asburyseminary.edu

asbury.to/firstfruits

41ST INTERNATIONAL CHRISTIAN ENDEAVOR Convention

GRAND RAPIDS, MICHIGAN

JULY 9-15, 1951

Official

Report

BUILD WITH CHRIST

HOMER A. RODEHEAVER   B. D. ACKLEY

Build with Christ, Our on-ly sure foun-da-tion,

Build with Christ, To save our church and na-tion,

Build with Christ, The Rock of our sal-va-tion,

On this Rock we will build with Christ.

41st Convention

of the

International Society

of

Christian Endeavor

•

Grand Rapids, Michigan

July 9-15, 1951

• •

Edited by
Raymond M. Veh, D.D.

• • •

Printed by the
International Society of
Christian Endeavor
1201 East Broad St., Columbus 5, Ohio

1

Contents

Illustrations

Convention Photographs

Pictures of convention scenes and personalities in this official report were taken by Peter Verburg, official convention photographer, and Earl Spielmacher.

CONVENTION CHIEFS

Clyde W. Meadows, D.D.
Chairman, International
Convention Program
Committee

Jacob H. Tigelaar
General Chairman
Grand Rapids Convention
Committee

Louis H. Benes, D.D.
Co-chairman
at
Grand Rapids

OUR PRESIDENTS

Daniel A. Poling, D.D., LL.D
President, World's Christian
Endeavor Union

Ernest R. Bryan, Litt D.
President, International
Society of Christian
Endeavor

STAFF OFFICERS
of the INTERNATIONAL SOCIETY

Harold E. Westerhoff
Administrative Secretary

Gene Stone, D.D.
General Secretary

Rev. Charles E. F. Howe
Associate General Secretary
and Treasurer

3

THE WHITE HOUSE
WASHINGTON

Dear Dr. Bryan:

Hearty greetings to the Christian Endeavorers from all parts of North America as you meet in your forty-first convention in Grand Rapids. I understand that you are observing the seventieth anniversary of the founding of the Christian Endeavor movement as you meet this year. May your next seventy years be as fruitful as the last in challenging young people with the Christian way of life.

It was my pleasure to send greetings to you when you met in Toronto two years ago and to cable my prayerful thoughts to your Christian comrades from twenty-four different countries (including even some from behind the iron curtain) when your world leaders met in London last summer. The challenge of world communism which faced us then is still before us and I would urge that you give great thought to what Christian young people and their leaders in our great democracies of Canada and the United States can do to stem the tide of Godless materialism which the imperialists of the Kremlin have launched upon a world that wants to be peaceful.

I was glad to learn that at Grand Rapids you are inaugurating a Crusade for Christian Citizenship and that you are out to combat communism in all its forms, crime in our municipalities and wherever else it is found, and civic indifference which is one of our most serious handicaps. As we build our defenses for whatever may happen on the world front, we must also build a strong and alert citizenry at home. We need more citizens who are willing and eager to work at the job of being good citizens. Your program will help to do exactly that.

May God's richest blessing be upon you as you meet to plan for service as Christian youth and leaders of young people in the critical days ahead.

Very sincerely yours,

(signed) Harry S. Truman

Dr. Ernest R. Bryan,
President,
International Society of Christian Endeavor,
3829 Cathedral Avenue, N.W.,
Washington 16, D. C.

4

CHAPTER I

As the Day Dawned

JULY smiled with all its warmth and brilliance. By auto, bus, train and plane delegates poured into the Furniture Capital of the World. Grand Rapids, Michigan, turned its best face to Christian Endeavorers who came from almost forty states of the union, two provinces of Canada and from nations as far away as India. Officials of the Convention Committee, pages, hotel clerks and citizens wore their gayest smiles to greet the delegates.

Some of the officials and their families had come to the headquarters' city for pre-convention meetings. There had been advance meetings of the Executive Committee of the International Society of Christian Endeavor, the Committee on United Strategy, the Finance Committee and other groups. Over the week-end these gatherings had been secluded in committee rooms, but Monday, July 9, there was a subconscious feeling that big things were about to happen. The Civic Auditorium found workmen setting up a beautiful platform setting, the book store displaying the latest books and essential Christian Endeavor materials, the Exhibit Hall housing all kinds of elaborate displays.

One group of delegates went about with an "I know my way" certainty. These were the people who had attended the 36th International Convention of Christian Endeavor held in Grand Rapids in 1937. Then there were others who, like Dr. Daniel A. Poling, could hark back to conventions held 40 years ago. For the most part, however, the delegates were young people, many of them high schoolers. They were all alert to the thrilling opportunities that a new place and an unexperienced international gathering might hold for them.

By 6:30 p.m. delegates were ready to engage in the pre-convention service of prayer. This was held in the Black and Silver Room of the Civic Auditorium. Jacob H. Tigelaar, Grand Rapids Convention Committee chairman, presided. Well-chosen choruses were sung—"He Lives," "Into My Heart," "Build With Christ." Rev. George C. Douma, pastor Calvary Reformed Church, Grand Rapids, gave a brief meditation. He urged the delegates to make the most of this Convention by being mindful of the Presence of Christ and open to the leadership of the Holy Spirit.

CHAPTER II

The Curtain Rises

CONVENTIONS are an old story to Christian Endeavor.

Yet there is an unusual thrill as a new Convention opens. The air of anticipation is sufficient to make delegates want to be in their seats on time. Delegations carry their banners and plant them at designated places. Colorful costumes make visitors watch oncoming groups of delegates. State songs and religious choruses are flung across the convention hall. Unmistakably, an event of exceptional significance is about to begin. The very air tingles.

The organ starts, with echoes of the piano accompanying the majestic instrument. Then the lights are turned on more strongly. An expectant hush falls on the assembly. Then the soft green curtain rises and the 300-voice chorus choir in white and black is framed by the fluted columns of the platform. The lights play on the 12 foot white cross banked with palms on the one side of the platform, and then on the flags of the nations at the other side. Floral tributes in red, white and blue flowers give richness to the setting.

President Ernest R. Bryan officially calls the convention into session and introduces General Secretary Gene Stone to preside for the evening. Officers of the International Society are greeted with applause. Then Rev. Lester H. Case, the official song leader, leads the convention in a rousing service of song. The convention theme chorus "Build With Christ" is learned. The convention chorus sings as if it had sung together for years. Welcome is extended by Mr. Porter, representing Mayor Paul C. Goebel, of the city of Grand Rapids. Miss Eunice Nelson, a charming young person, gives a sincere witness to the meaning of Christ for her life. Carol Bryan, our International Society President's daughter, leads the period of devotional meditation as printed in the program. Jack White, president of Grand Rapids C. E. Union, leads in prayer. The 41st International Convention of Christian Endeavor is under way.

Two messages were presented in this great opening service. The first, by the movement's president, is printed in full, because it set the keynote for the convention.

Said Dr. Ernest R. Bryan:

> On one of the rolling hills of Northern Virginia overlooking the city of Washington, an inspiring work of art will soon be lifted up to the glory of the defenders of democracy at Iwo Jima. This impressive statue, wrought of ten tons of bronze, will be 122 feet or 4 stories high and will be seen from 60 miles away. Oncoming generations will come to *view* this work of art, *walk* by the massive figures, and *think* again of the heroic Marines and sailors who lifted the colors on the strategic heights of Mount Suribachi on the south side of the tiny island which was bought at the price of 5,563 valiant men killed in action and 17,343 wounded. Iwo Jima will long live on in man's memory

because at that place during the crucial hours of a great struggle, in the words of Admiral Nimitz, "uncommon valor was a common virtue." That phrase too will live on. When we think of uncommon valor, we shall think of Iwo Jima for there it reached the heights. Joe Rosenthal, the A.P. photographer, who made the greatest picture of World War II, and Felix deWeldon, as the sculptor, who has preserved that moment for all time, have done something for all of us. Uncommon valor may thus become a more common virtue.

Another scene now comes to mind. It is a statue on a busy street in the busy city of London. It is the sculptured likeness of a heroine of World War I, a noble person who gave her life in the service of her country as she engaged voluntarily in a dangerous mission. As she was about to be shot by her enemy captors, she gave to the world this phrase, "Patriotism is not enough." Indeed, Edith Cavell gave us more than an example, more than a phrase, she gave us a great expression to a great idea—love of humanity that goes beyond mere patriotism. On that stone monument in the heart of the throbbing city of London, we find these undying words, "Patriotism is not enough." When we visited London for the World's Christian Endeavor Convention last summer, some of us stopped to view the life-size statue and the inscription and think about the meaning of it all. Somehow it reminds one of an earlier scene in the drama of human events, a scene where the human blended with the divine to mark a turning point in the history of life on this planet.

And now we turn to that earlier scene. It is on a hill far away and yet somehow it seems very close. The time is more than 1900 years ago, but it is so vivid that it seems very recent. We were not there but we are closely related to it . . . yes, we are part of that scene, you may even feel that you were there. For the central figure in that scene, uncommon valor was not enough, patriotism was not enough, devotion to the highest of ideals was not enough. There was a love of humanity so great and so broad that the blameless one who shouldered mankind's wrongdoings was indeed a citizen of the world, founder of universal brotherhood. He was and is a community leader whose community and whose leadership transcend time and distance. Across the hills and valleys of time, we can see him and we hear him saying, *"Greater love hath no man than this."*

This scene includes a cross and above that cross is a sign, crudely inscribed. It says, "This is the King" and it says it in three languages—Latin, Greek, and Hebrew. How significant and how symbolic! He is King of Kings and Lord of All. "This is the King"—it says in Greek, the language of culture and knowledge—great art, great philosophy, great thoughts. "This is the King"—it says in Latin, the language of government and law and order—great conquests, great codes of justice, great administrative achievement. "This is the King"—it says in Hebrew, the language of religion—great words of life, great deeds, great objectives, great souls.

It was on that cross that religion reached its highest expression. Mere religion in itself is not enough. It has to be applied to the needs of humanity. It has to be personalized in the words of the Christ who died on the cross to have its fullest expression. He is the King of life—all of life—and, as one translator has it, he is the pioneer of life.

Put these elements of uncommon virtue, devotion beyond patriotic expectation, and the elements of culture, knowledge, government, and religion at its best all together, and we have Christian Citizenship. Under Christ, it is a form of citizenship that has a concern for all humanity and for each individual belonging to the human family. It embodies valor, patriotism, culture, and knowledge of people and states. It embodies law and government. It embodies religion as the soul turns toward God, as creator and Heavenly Father.

Let us think on some of these things.

Uncommon valor is needed today to successfully fight two wars—the war against communism and the war against all other forms of crime. I say "other" advisedly because communism is one of the greatest crimes ever to beset the human race. With its perverted logic, its diabolical cunning, its enslavement of the human mind and spirit and with frequently the destruction of the body as well as the soul, communism is our No. 1 enemy.

Nor can these other crimes escape our attention. We are especially concerned now about crimes against and by high schoolers. The narcotics peddlers are claiming not hundreds, but thousands, of victims among teen-agers. The use of dope leads to other crimes too hideous to mention, but these crimes of degredation can not be ignored. The vitality, the self-respect, the character of our young people—our continent's most valuable possession—are at stake. The Kefauver committee showed us what is happening in many of our cities. The unholy alliance of crime and politics must be broken. Civic pride must be fostered. Police protection must be expanded and improved. Teen-agers must be given an opportunity to grow up in communities that are safe. Examples of civic virtue, not moral decline, should be there to guide and inspire. We must build for a better today and for better tomorrows in this matter of Christian citizenship.

Wishful thinking is not enough. A negative attitude of mere condemnation of unwholesome conditions will not change matters much. Even an expanded program of social services will not completely meet the desperate needs which confront us. The approach must be positive, the program must be far-reaching; the objectives must be Christian. When the noted architect and engineer of the 19th century, Daniel H. Burnham, said, "make no little plans," he uttered a profound admonition for this day as well as for the young people of his day.

The plans must be big. The challenge is inescapable. Our duty is clear. In the words of Mordecai, that defender of the downtrodden and oppressed peoples in ancient Persia, "Who knows but thou art come to the kingdom for such a time as this?" We can think seriously about our Christian Endeavor movement and its possibilities today. And who knows but that our organization has been led of God to this moment, for such a time as this, for a great purpose. If we will, we can with God's guidance spearhead a movement for Christian citizenship that will change many of the prevailing ways of life on this continent. This land could be Christian. This land can be ruled by lofty thinkers and careful planners, by unselfish leaders, by citizens who take upon themselves the labors as well as the benefits of citizenship. In the struggle for men's minds hearts' uncommon valor can wipe out the strangleholds of the underworld. An alert citizenry can replace the present apathy. The spirit of the Christ can replace the selfish interests and the chiselers at the economic and political council tables. It is men's minds and hearts that must be reached. Citizenship, like health, must be sought. It must be accompanied by the will to get better, to do better. Outside palliatives are not enough. There must be a change inside.

And what can we do? First of all, we can decide individually and collectively that we are going to do something—and something big starting with ourselves. Then we can inform, we can educate, we can agitate for better conditions in our cities and towns, states, nations, and provinces. We can organize. We can enlist the interest and support of others. We can publicize. In the best sense of the term, we can propagandize. And, as Christians, we have the greatest of all channels open to us—the channel of prayer. The prayer power of this group here could bring miracles to pass. We know that prayer changes things. And we have some things in our political system that need to be changed. And we need to do some sacrificing to change them. The good citizen works at the job of being a good citizen, as the President of the United States has pointed out in his letter to this convention. The good citizen must be informed, he must take the time to go out and enlist the help and the votes of others if this democracy is going to work. And the best answer to communism is a democracy that works for its people and a people that work for a common good. We must dive into the dirty business of politics and clean it up. This is no side-lines operation. We must get into the thick of the game and see that it is played right, that it is a clean game.

Specifically, we launch here at the Grand Rapids Convention a Crusade for Christian Citizenship, and we mean every word of that phrase. It is a *crusade*, it is *"for"* something; it is *Christian*; and *citizenship*, our goal, means duties and responsibilities as well as rights and privileges. We are setting up a Department of Christian Citizenship in the International Society with Director Charles Howe in charge. We are asking the states and provinces to set up similar departments in their unions. We are outlining goals and objectives along with pointing out methods and techniques for societies and other youth groups. We are inaugurating training courses. We are issuing helpful literature. We hope to set up some demonstration centers. We are planning to exchange ideas and experiences and keep everybody fully informed. We are all set to do pertinent research, investigate certain conditions, and do some straight-from-the-shoulder reporting on conditions and needs. We are seeking special funds and additional personnel *We are making no little plans.*

While enroute to the world's convention of Christian Endeavor in Berlin several years ago, I left Venice, Italy, in a plane which was bound for Munich, Germany, and from there I was to go on to Hamburg, where I was to meet a party of North American Endeavors and escort them to Oberammergau, site of the Passion Play. The little plane had a forced landing in Bolzano, a picturesque village nestled amid the mountains of northern Italy, in the Dolomites area of the Tyrol. After an exasperating delay, we set off again. We were up about 35 minutes and had to turn back to Bolzano. The atmospheric pressure was such that we could not get over the mountains. I thought at one time that we might just as well pick out a good one and hit it and be done with it. That thought did not remain long, however, because we had an objective, an important goal we wanted to reach—it was Oberammergau where we would see the stirring events of the last week of our Saviour's life re-enacted for our inspiration. After we landed again in Bolzano, one of the three passengers found an automobile of doubtful background and ability. We set off on the road to the north, around the dangerous curves, dodging animals, people, and vehicles of all descriptions and some beyond description. We made it as far as Innsbruck by this precarious method; took a train to Munich; another train to Hamburg, met the ship; escorted the people to Oberammergau and saw that inspiring drama, greatest of dramas of the greatest of lives—the story of the King of all life.

Sometimes we may not be able to soar over the mountains. The atmosphere around us may hold us down, but we can go forward by means of transportation and communication that are available to us. There is a way and that way will be opened to us. Whatever the barriers, we press onward "trusting in the Lord Jesus Christ for strength" toward that day when the kingdoms of the earth shall become the kingdoms of our Lord. His citizens we are and Him do we serve as we engage in a mighty Crusade for Christian Citizenship.

Bishop William J. Walls Speaks

The second notable address of this first session was given by Bishop William J. Walls, presiding bishop of the African Methodist Episcopal Zion Church, Chicago, Illinois. Speaking on "Christian Devotion and Loyalty" Bishop Walls said:

"Loyalty to Jesus is split between political division, and the church that seeks to go beyond it or seeks points of common agreement and Christian relations or understanding is suspected by the West and charged by the East of betraying ideological inviolates. Youth of the generation are thus handicapped in seeking loyalty to Christ that leads beyond set boundaries of troubled times. But, amidst all this, there are those who have not lost hope. This new price-setting to be a Christian was due to come. Modern Christian education had grown soft in its reduction of religion to an agency of giving satiation for satisfaction and comfort for courage. It is difficult to get a real tart and tasty apple because hybridizing has made all apples sweet. So it, the scientific attitude, has made all standards of religion and character building sweet and indulgent. But, now again must Christians become bold to find joy in suffering with Christ if he would reign with Him . . .

Bishop William J. Walls

"Loyalty has two levels. Viz. (1) loyalty to the status quo and (2) loyalty to the great reality. The majority have perhaps neither ability nor courage to blaze new trails. Such ones do well to follow with wise caution and loyalty the highway of the accepted beliefs and organization. After all, organized life and mutual growth are achieved in this way where the common run of people live. This may be only salvation, growth or self-realization. But, when we build with Christ, we, in steering youth, must not forget His right not only to conform but also to independence to follow His own inspired lead. Dominatin defeats that very purpose and too often stunts moral growth and spiritual discovery.

"The higher level of living is creative. The ideal is to follow *Christ as a moving point* who says, 'You do not know all now, but follow me to know more hereafter.'

This is the holy dare. Christ lived the ideal incisive life. He respected old mores only so far as they measured up to ever emerging truth and freedom to pursue reality. He followed God from within and broke with the vogue where God and truth led Him. However, this activity within must have also, control to effect external experiences and establish social conduct. 'If he be a person,' says Frank Herriott, 'he must maintain that inner citadel of integrity.'

"Loyalty to the church means down with Communism with its Atheism and up with Democracy, chastized and Christianized when all shall come to know the Lord from the least to the greatest, when the day of the sun of peace shall dawn and the shadows of conflict, the stench of slums and shambles and the greed of prosperity shall flee away."

Delegates and visitors fill Civic Auditorium to capacity.

Members of the Executive Committee and other leaders of International Society stand at the entrance of the headquarters' hotel.

Rev. Lester H. Case, convention song leader, directs singing from Civic Auditorium platform.

Press conference held with Dr. Billy Graham. Shown, left to right, are: Rev. Duane Reahm, Grand Rapids; Rev. Harland Steele, chairman, radio committee; Dr. Raymond M. Veh, editor, Builders; Dr. Gene Stone, general secretary, International C.E.; Dr. Clyde W. Meadows, vice president, International C.E.; Dr. Ernest R. Bryan, president, International C.E.; Dr. Louis H. Benes, editor, the Church Herald; Dr. Billy Graham; Winfield Caslow, Grand Rapids; Jacob H. Tigelaar, chairman, Grand Rapids convention, and Phyllis I. Rike, assistant to General Secretary of International C.E.

CHAPTER III

The First Full Day

THE observance of the Daily Quiet Hour is a Christian Endeavor habit. Promptly and reverently the delegates came by the hundreds into Civic Auditorium at 8:30 each morning to open the day with worship. In these hours the tone of the day was set. Here thoughts were planted to germinate in many days to come. Hymns sung quietly, a solo with a spiritual message, and a period for prayer made the Quiet Hour a time of uplift and prayer. Theme song for this period was "Till I Become Like Thee."

Dr. Jacob Prins, minister of Evangelism of the Reformed Church in America, of Grand Rapids, presented the basic essentials in "Building with Christ." On this first day he spoke on "That We May Know Him." He held that personal acquaintance with Jesus, the Saviour, is "the most meaningful experience in life." Quoting many scripture passages that reveal how men may know Christ and serve him, Dr. Prins laid deep spiritual foundations for personal building of lives that count.

Two hours of discussion and forum groups on techniques of Christian Endeavor work followed. These are reported in a separate chapter.

Then came the General Convention session in the big auditorium, broadcast over radio station WFUR. With Harold E. Westerhoff presiding, Rev. Charles E. F. Howe, Associate General Secretary and Treasurer, gave a timely messsage on "What Is Christian Stewardship?" "The motive of giving is absolute consecration," held Mr. Howe. "The great example of self-giving is Jesus himself . We are called to identify ourselves with his work through our gifts. Nothing is more dangerous to the soul than wealth. Money promises to make us almost gods in power and influence. But if money is misused it tends to make greed grow until the spiritual values in life are almost crowded out."

During the afternoon, a Luncheon for State and National Christian Endeavor Union officers, the Board of Trustees meeting, and a tea with officers of the World C. E. Union, International Society of Christian Endeavor trustees and members of the Grand Rapids Convention Committee in the receiving line followed one on top of the other. Norman Klauder, Philadelphia, later presided over a dinner for trustees, program leaders and officers honoring informally Mrs. Joseph Holton Jones. Many Endeavorers visited the Book Store and the exhibit hall during the interim between sessions.

AT 7:45 p.m. the curtain went up on the platform to again reveal the great convention choir. Rev. J. Wesley Siebert. Canadian Christian Endeavor

Dr. Jacob Prins   Dr. Frank F. Warren

Union president, presided over the service following the song period directed by Lester Case. Dr. Raymond M. Veh, chairman of the Committee on Resolutions, presented a resolution adopted by the Convention calling for the establishment of a Crusade for Christian Citizenship and setting up a department in this field for the International Society, state and provincial unions. Springing to his feet Dr. Daniel A. Poling supported this move and raised $4,000 for the undergirding of the department.

Guy P. Leavitt, Editor of *The Lookout*, of the Standard Publishing House, Cincinnati, Ohio, presented the seven winners of free trips and expenses to the Convention for their activity in local church Christian Endeavor societies. These young people received a fine ovation.

After worship Mary Lou Poorman gave her testimony in sweet and simple terms. Dr. Frank F. Warren, president of Whitworth College, Spokane, Washington, addressed the large audience on "The Master Life." He said.

"The Master Life is the crucified life. Christianity is the only religion in the world that starts with a cross. It is only as it continues in the shadow of that cross that it becomes worldwide in its influence. Paul is the greatest example the world has ever known of a man who said that he had been crucified (Gal. 2 20) and yet who continued to live victoriously. Once he hated the cross, but finally the spirit of mighty Saul of Tarsus descended from the throne room of his heart and ascended to that cross until he could say, 'I am crucified with Christ.'

"Secondly, the Master Life is a constrained life. It was Paul himself who declared that the 'love of Christ constraineth us.' The Master Life is conscious of a mighty constraining love—a love that can hold but also a love that can impel, a love that embraces but a love that expels. There is no force in all the world so great as the constraining love of Christ. The Master Christian is one who is held in the mighty grip of a world-embracing love. You can't escape it, and it drives you beyond yourself, out of yourself, and into the lives of others.

"In the third place, the Master Life is a commissioned life. One living the Master Life is always living a life of service. We realize that we are workers with Christ, and because we have been crucified with Christ and constrained by His love, there comes the sense of commission, of partnership, and we go out into the world not to represent ourselves, our little causes, and our warped philosophies, but as partners with Christ to represent Him. This same Christ who said, 'Come unto me,' also said, 'He that believeth on me . . . from within him shall flow rivers of living water.' So the Master Life is not a life of limited resources but of overflowing capacities. It is filled with a dominating purpose, and the difference between the achievers and the non-achievers in our world is not a difference of intellect, education, or opportunity but of purpose. The world has no greater need today than for the rising of a solid phalanx of young people commissioned by Christ to go out into a world and proclaim Him.

"Fourth, the Master Life is a conquered life. Paul said, 'the life which I now live in the flesh I live by the faith of the Son of God, who loved me, and gave Himself for me.' Only to the degree that one has been conquered by Christ does he himself conquer. The Master Life conquers in the realm of personal conflict. You cannot conquer in the arena of the world until you have conquered in the arena of your own heart. The Master Life also conquers in the realm of endeavor Even as Paul two thousand years ago became the great Master Christian of his century, so you may become a Master Christian in this century until you can finally say with Paul, 'I can do all things through Christ who strengtheneth me.'"

With lights extinguished, and a spotlight focussed on the cross with youth kneeling at the base, Dr. Clyde W. Meadows called the delegates and audience to lift their spiritual sights. It was a moment of high inspiration.

At the close of the session, as each evening, when a full day of activities had been the lot of every delegate, the young people went quickly to the worship services of the state and regional groups. This was in the great tradition of Christian Endeavor conventions. Many leaders were utilized in these periods and hundreds of delegates participated in the prayer periods.

Rev. George C. Douma
assistant chairman of program committee, introduces
Dr. Graham to overflow
audience.

Many exhibits were appreciated by the delegates. Here is the striking display of the Kansas
Union with Maxine Bond, associate president of
the Sunflower Union, viewing it.

The fine group of usherettes at the convention who served in a friendly and efficient
manner at mass meetings.

CHAPTER IV

Into the Long Stride

WEDNESDAY found the delegates wending their way to the Civic Aud- itorium in good time to prepare themselves for the Quiet Hour. Using the scene of "The Transfiguration of Christ," Dr. Prins portrayed the dramatic possibilities of this event. The disciples who were with Jesus after the thrilling, heart-searching event went down to the valley to begin to build knowing that Jesus is God's beloved son in whom He is well-pleased. God presented Jesus to mankind that we might truly know Him. If we of this generation really desired to know Him the multitudes would not drink and carouse and dissipate God-given energies. We would honor Him with complete consecration of self and through exaltation of His Gospel.

Following the usual round of conference periods the Morning Assembly brought three special speakers. First was Dr. Frederick W. Cropp, General Secretary of the American Bible Society, New York. He evidenced the far-reaching work of this agency devoted to dissemination of the Scriptures to the needy and under-privileged around the world. Of unusual interest was the displaying of a plaque sent to the Society recently by Korean Christian soldiers. It was made out of tin cans and scraps of metal collected on the battlefield. The cross was central in the plaque design with tributes to Christ and the Church inscribed thereon.

Dr. Norman W. Paullin, pastor Baptist Temple, Philadelphia, Pa., gave the major presentation on "What Is the Quiet Hour?"

He held that:

"First of all, the quiet hour is an essential part of Christian Endeavor. It has been in our program from the very beginning. It is a portion of our Christian Endeavor pledge.

"Secondly, it is a 'privilege' and a 'trust.' The quiet hour follows our personal commitment to Jesus Christ. It is a part of the 'Master Life.' If we really love Him we will spend time in His presence.

"Thirdly, it is best stated as:

1. A set time.
2. With a specific purpose.
3. In a definite place.
4. Involving two persons.

"The quiet hour has a Scripture foundation in Matthew 6:6. 'But thou, when thou prayest, enter into thy closet, and when thou hast shut thy door, pray to thy Father which is in secret, and thy Father which seeth in secret shall reward thee openly.'

Dr. Norman W. Paullin

"A. 'When thou'—*a set time*. This is one of the 'first things.' Every Christian must and can find time for daily worship.

"B. 'When thou prayest'—*a specific purpose*. In this quiet time of prayer and meditation, we express our love and we tell our needs. In the reading of the Word and quietness He expresses His love and gives guidance and direction.

"C. 'Enter into thy closet'—*a definite place*. It may be anywhere, but we must find a place. Just as we must open the door to Him, so it is our responsibility to shut the door—to *shut out* and to *shut in*.

"D. 'Pray to thy Father'—*two persons*. This means 'my God and I.' "

15

The third presentation was by Chaplain (Brigadier General) Fred C. Reynolds, of Washington, D. C., who explained the new united approach of the churches to provide religious expression for the 3,500,000 men of the United States in national service. This is to be known as "The United Fellowship of Protestants." Christian Endeavor will be a part of 'the important approach which is approved by the chaplains of the three branches of the armed services and under the supervision of the Commission on Protestant Chaplains.

Luncheons this noon were for leaders working with Junior age children, and another for annual members of the International Society.

The big activity for the afternoon outside of the meeting of the Corporation of the International Society, was the outing trip to Ottawa Beach on Lake Michigan. A caravan of 150 cars took delegates to the lake. Mother Nature did not favor the delegates with a bright day, but the trip proved exciting for the delegations and the fellowship at the beach was typically Christian Endeavor.

Dr. Meadows, Dr. Graham and Dr. Stone

CHAPTER V

For Fun and Frolic and Fervor

WHAT a banquet! Everybody was dressed in their best "bib and tucker." Some were in formals that swept the floor of the lower convention hall. Some were in sweaters and others in state regalia. But all came with hopes of a night of fun and seriousness. And for four hours that is what everyone had.

First came the food. Fifteen churches cooperated to prepare food that the delegates might enjoy a banquet at a reasonable price. Seconds were available on most everything. One hundred and thirty men and women of the churches served the food in record time. No one could have seen a finer demonstration of the ecumenical spirit than in that meal.

Then came none other than Arch McQuilkin, dubbed by Dr. Dan Poling as "the Will Rogers of Christian Endeavor." With a store of humor and a knowledge of how to wield a crowd into unity, the 1,014 banqueters laughed until they often cried. Lester Case led in familiar ballads climaxing with "Sing, sing, sing for the singing" from "The Chocolate Soldier." Jack Boeskool gave two solos accompanied by Mrs. Franklin Van Buren. Stuart Noordyk was at the organ for the singing.

Dr. Gene Stone aided by Carroll M. Wright, former Associate Secretary and Treasurer of Christian Endeavor, and Harold Westerhoff made 10 awards to states and provinces rating high in registrations. Ohio won first prize for advance registrations with Wisconsin winning second honors. State delegations also recognized winners of "The Lookout" contest as again presented by Guy P. Leavitt.

The three youth addresses were on "Build with Christ Through Christian Citizenship." Edith Brouwer emphasized the need for strengthening family relationships, particularly through daily family worship, the wise use of Sunday, and personal witness. Harold Davidson, Columbus, Ohio, took the crisis of material civilization as a springboard for discussing the challenge, opportunity and responsibility to build Christian citizenship. An active obedience to Jesus Christ is the only basis for building a better world. Christian citizenship implies devotion and love to God, to fellowmen and to one's country. This can be fulfilled through young people of this day who accept this as a public responsibility.

Jack Graf, of Mercedes, Texas, spoke "On Overcoming Prejudices." Recalling the constitutional provisions of this nation for recognition of people of all classes and color, the denial of such privileges is both unAmerican and unChristian, he said. Christian Endeavor recognizes no barriers of race or class and thus becomes a positive factor in overcoming prejudices.

High moment of the evening came in the presentation by Dr. Poling of the International Youth's Distinguished Service Citation to Mrs. Joseph Holton Jones. Mrs. Jones, in response, said: "I feel that my debt will never be paid

17

to Christian Endeavor." Then she traced her development through Christian Endeavor societies, conventions and contacts to the depths of spiritual power which she now possesses. "Everything that I remember that has stayed with me I have learned through Christian Endeavor," said Mrs. Jones.

"It has been the practice of Christian Endeavor to welcome any group into its fellowship and has been ecumenical in spirit," she continued. "I'm glad to belong to an organization that stands for the principles of interracial fellowship. I feel my greatest Alma Mater of all is Christian Endeavor. Receiving this citation is my diploma. I learned my geography the Christian Endeavor way. Youth without training and discipline cannot be relied on. But with faith in Christ, youth hold the key to the future."

The huge cross dominated the impressive
platform setting.

Radio Broadcast

Dr. Ernest R. Bryan
presides at service from
the studios of Station
WJEF, Grand Rapids.
which was broadcast
over the network of the
Columbia Broadcasting
System July 15. Dr.
Daniel A. Poling is
ready to begin his ad-
dress.

Conference Leaders and Speakers at Convention

Members of the faculty for the "school" at the International Christian Endeavor
gathering as shown as follows:

First row (left to right)—Harold E. Davidson, Rev. Earle W. Gates, Rev. Donald
D. Abbey, Robert S. Hildreth, B. McClain Cochran, Rev. Lester H. Case, Phil C.
Reed, Rev. Brenton J. K. Arthur, Galen Colclesser, Rev. John F. Little, Rev. R. Ward
Williams, Dr. Norman W. Paullin, and Rev. Ezekiel F. Albert.

Second row (left to right)—Rev. Henry Bast, Mrs. Alice Griffin, Minnie Bittner,
Christina E. MacAskill, Dr. Gene Stone, Dr. Clyde W. Meadows, Ernest S. Marks,
Lois B. Ludowic, Margaret Paugh, Viroqua Nodolf, Phyllis I. Rike, and Mrs. Ezekiel
F. Albert.

Third row (left to right)—Rev. Wellington H. Whittlesey, Dr. R. W. Rash, Rev.
Henry C. Jacobs, Dr. Raymond M. Veh. Rev. J. Clinton Hoggard, Rev. J. Wesley
Siebert, Dr. Ernest R. Bryan, Rev. Clair E. Beatty, Dr. Elmer Becker, Charles O.
Heyward, Rev. George C. Douma, Paul F. Hurley, Julian Moran, and Rev. Elwood
Dunn.

Mrs. Joseph Holton Jones

is the t[...] [recipi]ent of

International Youth [Di]stinguished Service Citation

and the first wom[an to be] honored with this

Award

Mrs. Jones is Vice President of the International Society of Christian Endeavor and a member of the Executive Committee of the World's Christian Endeavor Union. By her travels into all areas of the world where Christian Endeavor activities center, by her participation in conferences and conventions, and her constructive interest in the development of youth programs, by her generous support of Christian Endeavor in the crisis years and beyond, she has become, as no other living leader among us,

"Mrs. Christian Endeavor."

But the interests of this gracious, talented and selfless woman have not been confined to Christian Endeavor. To her community and church, at home and abroad, as President of the Wilmington New Century Club and in responsible positions with the Federation of Women's Clubs, the Council of Churches, and in many denominational activities, she has been and is identified with vital organizations and programs, civic and social as well as religious.

Helen Lyon Jones is a prodigal steward of her time, money and life. In her giving, her right hand knows not the left but her wisdom to decide, matches her heart to bestow.

This Award is the unanimous expression of the love, esteem and gratitude of her associates in the executive leadership of the International Society of Christian Endeavor and the World's Christian Endeavor Union.

Daniel A. Poling

Jane Stone   *Ernest K. Byam*

Grand Rapids, Michigan, July [...] 19[...]

**Facsimile of International Youth's
Distinguished Service Citation.**

INTERNATIONAL YOUTH'S DISTINGUISHED
SERVICE CITATION

Mrs. Joseph Holton Jones

For the first time in the bestowing of five International Youth's Distinguished Service Awards at as many conventions of our movement, the Award this year went to a woman. Mrs. Jones is Vice-President of the International Society of Christian Endeavor, and is a member of the Executive Committee of the World's Christian Endeavor Union. She has traveled to conventions held abroad, has generously supported the movement, and has faithfully served her community and church in loyal service.

Previous recipients of the citation are Rear Admiral Richard E. Byrd, Herbert Hoover, former President of the United States; Dr. Harold E. Stassen, President, University of Pennsylvania; and Dr. Daniel A. Poling, President of the World's Christian Endeavor Union.

CHAPTER VI

Mid-Way

ERNEST S. MARKS in the Faculty Breakfast reminded the group leaders and speakers that this was the half-way day of the convention. With the background of three good days there were to be three more greater days of convention program and spirit. And, to ·be sure, the Convention spirit was mounting to make this one of the memorable conventions of the 70 years of history of the Christian Endeavor movement.

Quiet Hour moved to the Black and Silver auditorium which made for more intimate family spirit. Dr. Prins reminded the group that "there is no substitute for knowing Jesus." "Drifting is a dangerous thing, but very easy." Treating the familiar saying of Jesus, "If any man hear my sayings and does them he is like the man who built his house on a rock," the speaker held that "we must listen to Jesus,

1. For he is God and ought to be obeyed; 2. We belong to him; 3. We ought to do what he says because of what he is trying to do through us. Jesus thus must have the central place in every person's heart; we must study his Word to know what he is saying. We must pray to learn to know his will; we must be engaged in constructive Christian living."

Following the Educational Conference periods which were now rounding out a pattern of group sharing of problems, ideas and plans, the delegates met promptly at 11:30 o'clock for the Assembly broadcast over station WFUR. Harold E. Westerhoff presided and Lester Case with an impromptu choir led in inspirational singing.

Dr. Frank F. Warren, Spokane, Washington, presented the morning address on "Volunteers—Wanted."

"Something about volunteering for God's work gives power," Dr. Warren stated. "The plus element comes into the life that is wholly dedicated to Christian service." He pled that young people not live "small lives." "You can't be lazy and be Christian," he stated. Outlining the many Christian vocations open to young people he proposed the four choices young people can make: (1) to run away from life; (2) to run with life; (3) to run your own life; (4) to take life and turn it over to God.

Denominational luncheons were the order of the day for Thursday noon and afternoon. Around 15 denominational groups met in local Grand Rapids churches or in hotel or YM-YWCA dining rooms. This denominational fellowship is one of the anticipated experiences of the convention.

High-schoolers held a "hey-day" at John Ball Park enjoying the zoo and planned games and sports. The Youth Assembly also held its picnic in mid-afternoon.

Convention Hall Overflows

"THIS is my story, This is my song," 6,000 voices pealed forth in the old song as the great night of the convention opened. Clifford Barrows, the renowned song leader, directed the thrilling singing with Ted Smith at the piano. Beverly Shea sang, "It is no secret, what God can do for you." Then the curtains opened on the huge Convention Choir while all united in singing "All Hail the Power of Jesus' Name."

Warren Hoopes, Jr., of Pennsylvania, led the worship service aided by Frances Becker. Beverly Shea again sang "I'd Rather Have Jesus than Silver or Gold." Ted Smith played a brilliant offertory solo. Harold Davidson gave the youth witness in a beautifully-stated testimony. The chorus choir rendered the anthem, "Lift Up Your Voices."

Then Rev. George Douma introduced the one-time Christian Endeavor society president, now the world's leading evangelist, Billy Graham. Dr. Graham introduced Dr. Melvin Rosell, noted youth speaker. Beverly Shea followed singing, "I Saw One Hanging on a Tree."

Using the youthful years of the life of Moses as the basis for his sermon, Dr. Graham spoke on "Youth's Choice." He held that within the next forty minutes every young person must make a decision. He showed how youth living in an age of confusion could make his choice.

"Youth today are marching," stated Dr. Graham. "They are equipped with atomic weapons and can destroy the world and themselves if they do not have God. This is an age of intellectual failure. All the 'isms' have failed youth until they have nothing to hold on to. There is a restlessness among youth.

"Let's get into politics and clean up corruption. This is an age of political corruption and suicide. We are faced with a fanatical religion that is dedicated to destroy Christianity. To win the battle against Communism we have got to become as fanatical as the Communists over our belief in Christ. There is no hope to defeat Communism save through God.

"The greatest social program ever offered was outlined by Jesus in the Sermon on the Mount. There is no possibility under heaven of saving America until millions of youth are converted to Jesus Christ. It is an experience—a moment of decision— turning away from the past.

"Repentance means turning from the sins of the past, having faith in Christ and committing self to Him. It means loving Christ, following Christ, serving Christ. Christianity is a *do* religion until you don't have time for *don'ts*."

While the audience sang the familiar consecration hymn, "Have Thine Own Way," Dr. Graham made impassioned appeal for youth to accept Christ. In response to God's voice speaking through Dr. Graham 104 young people came to the front of the great auditorium, then moved to an adjoining room where Dr. Graham met them for prayer. It was a night never to be forgotten.

CHAPTER VII

Eventful Friday

DELEGATES were resolved to start each day right so the crowd at Quiet Hour seemed to grow day by day. After singing "Till I Become Like Thee," Dr. Prins resumed his deeply devotional presentations on the principles of building enduring lives. This morning his thesis was "If we would build with Christ we must exalt him. And I, if I be lifted up from the earth, will draw all manner of men unto me." "Jesus came to draw men back to God. It was God's plan that men should be reconciled to him through Christ. He did not say that He would draw men by His teachings or by His miracles. Only when He was lifted up on the cross in death for the propitiation of men's sins did He lay claim to men's loyalties. So He fulfills His promise by His glorious person, by means of the cross, and by His work and word."

Educational Conferences and the Youth Assembly caught up the basic truths of their discussions the next two hours. Then came the general convention session in the Black and Silver room. The morning was filled with promotion of various enterprises of the movement and singing that was lifting. Dr. Clyde W. Meadows spoke on the subject "How to Win Youth." He called young people to go into the community to carry the Gospel of Jesus Christ to high school mates, youth on the streets, and to indifferent members of the churches. The basic principles in winning youth he presented as follows:

1. Have a message to youth on the terribleness of sin and on the glorious salvation from sin which is possible through Christ Jesus.
2. Have a concern for youth.
3. Pray about unsaved youth.
4. Love youth to let them know His love.
5. Seek out youth.
6. Expect youth to respond.
7. Understand youth—their problems and attitudes and heart hungers.
8. Commit youth.
9. Use youth—give them a task, a place to work.

Regional state and provincial dinner conferences and several state union conventions filled the afternoon of this day. Junior Christian Endeavor leaders also shared experiences at one of the specially scheduled dinners.

FRIDAY evening with Rev. George C. Douma presiding found the hymn time of lifting value. The choir sang two selections, one *a cappella*. Then John McMillan, of Florida, led the worship with Marian Wales, Washington, D. C., giving the prayer. Dr. Raymond M. Veh, chairman of the Committee on Resolutions presented the results of the convention's group thinking with the delegates adopting the same. Then Marjorie Stiggers, Chicago, Ill., gave the youth testimony of faith in an effective manner.

"The Problem of Indecision"

FRIDAY evening's address by Dr. Norman W. Paullin on "The Problem of Indecision" climaxed this eventful day. Dr. Paullin held that

"The problems in the world are legion. The church is also beset by many problems. Perhaps the outstanding one is that of indecision. Too few are really wholeheartedly following Christ. While a relatively small number in America are anti-God and anti-church, multitudes remain undecided. The opposition forces (atheists and consecrated Christians) are kept from battle by the masses in the 'no man's land' of indecision.

"Christian Endeavorers can penetrate these millions—winning hundreds of thousands to Christ and the Church in these next two years. Revival fires are burning. Christian youth are in the forefront of this movement. For this we older folk thank God and take courage.

"The indifference to spiritual things can be broken down only by a personal demonstration of the Christ life. We must trust God for salvation and allow God to work that salvation out in life and practice.

"The millions of undecided must be challenged by facts and examples. The Old Testament story of the healing of Naaman gives the key—

(1) God had a prepared young person. (His example)
(2) God had a consecrated servant—a prophet. (Another exhibit)
(3) Definite instructions to be followed. (His facts)

As long as Naaman remained undecided, his problem grew steadily worse. When he trusted and obeyed, it was well with him.

"So it is with us and all those whom we long to see saved.

"Our task is great, the means adequate, and the results assured."

In an appeal for decisions for the 70th Anniversary Advance numbers made commitment in one or more of the following categories:

Trusting in the Lord Jesus Christ for strength I promise that I will strive to do whatever He would like to have me do and I hereby enroll in the 70th Anniversary Advance committing myself to the fundamental principles of Christian Endeavor: Confession of Christ, Loyalty to Christ's Church, Service for Christ, and Fellowship with Christ's People ....☐

I wish to become
A Comrade of the Quiet Hour ....☐
A member of the Tenth Legion ....☐
A Life Work Recruit ....☐
I will endeavor to win someone to Christ during this year ....☐
Becoming of voting age this year I pledge to vote as I believe a
Christian should ....☐

Twenty-five young people made first decisions for Christ and six for full-time Christian service, in addition to those who had made similar decisions the night previous.

This day closed as other nights with state and regional quiet hours bringing all delegates into a fellowship with Christ and each other.

CHAPTER VIII

Exciting Saturday

MANY more Endeavorers arrived from 1:00 a. m. on during this day from points as far distant as Toronto, Canada and Pittsburgh, Pennsylvania. Autos were crowded with weekenders who couldn't leave their work for weekday sessions but wouldn't miss a chance to be at an International Convention. Some brought material for parade floats and marchers.

All delegates were in the Black and Silver Room for the Morning Quiet Hour which again was addressed by Dr. Prins. This morning he spoke on "Bearing Witness to Him" as one of the essentials in "Building with Christ." Basing his message on John the Baptist, forerunner of Christ, Dr. Prins portrayed John as "a man with a great heritage, as one who let the sin of his generation weigh heavily on his heart, who had a great hope in the coming of the Christ to take man's sin away." So John records the marvelous truths to which "the Voice" called attention—to the person of Christ, His pre-existence, His pre-eminence, His presence, His great mission in the world, His emphasis on human responsibility to reveal their loyalty to God and prepare for the judgment of God. The effect of John's witness was to make men aware of the Presence among them, and to make them aware of the purpose of Christ's coming into the world. On that basis Dr. Prins called youth of this day to be "Voices for Christ" to prepare hearts for Christ's message.

This last day of Educational Conferences found groups making a last plunge into their respective subjects. Leaders made summaries of the week's thinking with preservation of constructive findings as found on page 41 of this Report.

At the General Convention session Rev. Ezekiel F. Albert widened the horizons of the delegates by speaking on "World Friendship." Basing his message on the country that is native to him, India, he portrayed the thrilling opportunities that are open to Christians to bring Christ to needy peoples. The hope of the future lies in Christians out-living and out-thinking the Communists. World friendship is impossible on any basis save that which is promised in the Gospel of Jesus Christ.

"Methods and means are not sufficient," said Rev. Albert. "The love and spirit of Christ are also needed . . . America has so much. If we do not feed the starving Communism will take over. Christ must be on our total experience. We must not only *live* the Gospel, we must *be* the Gospel."

The luncheon today permitted delegates to the World's Christian Endeavor Convention in London, England, in July 1950 to renew friendships established at that time.

CHAPTER IX

The Marching Throng

THOUSANDS of Grand Rapids citizens lined the sun-drenched streets of Grand Rapids to see the striking demonstration of the worldwide youth movement which is Christian Endeavor. Windows of stores and offices were lined with interested observers. Mayor Paul C. Goebel, other city officials, local church leaders, program participants, together with the judges, crowded the reviewing stand at Hotel Pantlind. It was a perfect day, warm, clear, and with a white cloud or two to break the monotony of the blue sky overhead.

Singing the hymns of the church and with banners and floats declaring allegiance to Christ, more than 3,000 young people followed Dr. Ernest Bryan, Dr. Daniel A. Poling, Dr. Gene Stone and other officers of Christian Endeavor at a brisk and hearty pace down the avenues. How the hosts of Endeavoring youth marched!

Leading the parade were nine motorcycle officers who rode their vehicles in the formation of a Cross. Following them came Grand Rapids Salvation Army Band playing "Onward Christian Soldiers."

Ohio Union was first in line of delegations because this Union attained the highest percentage of registration quotas for the Convention. The float carried an outline of the state of Ohio. In the center were large letters "CE." Wisconsin followed as second-place winners.

The Golden Rule Union of Washington, D. C., one of the most loyal unions in the movement through the years, was resplendent in white uniforms with blue and yellow capes.

In the parade Colorado's delegation evidenced the invitation to the International Society and all its friends to meet in Denver for the next Convention of the International Society in 1953.

The Illinois delegation attracted attention with marchers carrying red Christian Endeavor banners or red umbrellas with "Christian Endeavor" inscribed across the top. There was a hay wagon with delegates from Indiana. Iowa had a wagon load of Iowa beauties representing Christian Endeavor from that state. Observers also liked the Oklahoma "Indians."

Michigan, the home state, of course, had a great display. A 28-piece band with three majorettes and a drum major led the Michigan delegation. Finally after many beautiful floats and displays, there came delegate representatives of the city of Grand Rapids. In one group there were some 800 Junior Endeavorers all carrying colorful balloons.

When the parade was over everyone agreed, "It was the greatest parade, ever." The judges made their decisions and that night, in the Civic Auditorium, it was announced that Canada with its marching delegates led by the Union Jack and Christian flags and a Christian Endeavor banner, followed by representatives of the various Provinces, their occupations and trades (in dress) was the winner of first place on the basis of an original idea. The first place for "presentation" went to Illinois. In Michigan, first place went to the Muskegon Union for its idea of driving a wrecked car on the side of which read, "Does your life go like this? Build with Christ." The Golden Chain Union was among the award winners. The prize of first place for the local Grand Rapids Union went to Immanuel Reformed Church on the basis of their idea. Honorable mention to Fifth Reformed Church and first place to Grace Reformed Church on the basis of their presentation.

Many parades offer more gorgeous floats and count more bands in proportion to marchers, and more precision in marching order. But this parade was impressive—not because of elaborate and expensive display or painful hours of rehearsal. It impressed Grand Rapids people by the light in the eyes of the boys and girls and older friends who marched, by the certainty that here is a host of youth devoted to life's highest goals, that there is promise of a better world—a world in which constructive good will shall reign in the spirit of the living Christ. The parade was a sparkling demonstration of the ever youthful spirit of Christian Endeavor.

OUR FRIENDS FROM ABROAD

Rev. Ezekiel F. Albert   Mrs. Ezekiel F. Albert

The Pennsylvania delegation at the judges' stand.

Clever floats interested many thousands on the parade route. "More Than Conquerors" is prize-winning entry of Immanuel Reformed Church, Grand Rapids.

800 Junior Endeavorers formed one of the most enthusiastic portions of the parade.

CHAPTER X

Festival of Talent

AS THE Saturday evening feature Christian Endeavorers attending the convention participated in a Music Festival. The program was filled with solos, duets, and various musical presentations. B. McClain Cochran presided over the evening's session. The program was opened with singing directed by Rev. Lester H. Case.

A great thrill ran through the audience when Dr. Ernest R. Bryan read a telegram from Mr. Stanley Kresge of the Kresge Foundation of Detroit, Michigan, announcing the gift of $5,000 to Christian Endeavor to be used during the next year for the Christian Citizenship Crusade. Greetings were also received from the Seventh International Youth for Christ Meeting at Winona Lake, Indiana.

Devotions for the evening were brought by Thomas Thatcher with prayer by Maxine Bond. The new chairman of the Youth Assembly, Dick Pruiksma, was the Youth Witness for the occasion.

Solos were presented by Arthur Williams, South Bend, Indiana; Marilyn Bolks, Kalamazoo, Michigan; Jack Boeskool, Grand Rapids; and Thurman Rynbrandt, Grand Rapids, who also played a portion of his solo on the trombone.

Two accordion solos, one by Don Schlipp and the other by Clare Van Malsen were beautifully done. Both boys were from Grand Rapids.

Three young ladies from the host city who call themselves the "Mid-day Meditation Trio," brought a special number. They were Marcella Leestma, Helene Van Heest and Joan Van Heest.

Convention musicians, Kenneth Louis, organist, and Richard Bolks, pianist, did a wonderful job on a duet.

Two instrumental trios were also features of the evening's program. Purcell, John and Maurice Vandenburg brought music on the Spanish Guitar, Hawaiian Guitar and Accordion. A second trio composed of Ruth Jolman, Janet Wessels and Ruth Vandenberg played a selection on the violin, piano and clarinet.

The closing moments of meditation and prayer were brought by the World's President of Christian Endeavor, Dr. Daniel A. Poling.

CONFERENCE LEADERS

Virequa Nedelf   Dr. Elmer Becker   Mrs. Daniel A. Poling

CHAPTER XI

Climactic Sunday

A S IS invariably true, the Holy Communion Service at 8 o'clock on Sunday morning was for many Endeavorers the most sacred and memorable part of the Grand Rapids Convention. Christian Endeavorers in large numbers came to the Civic Auditorium to attend and share in the celebration of the Lord's Supper. Dr. Elmer Becker, president of Huntington College, Huntington, Ind., was the celebrant. Dr. S. S. Morris offered the prayer. Dr. John A. Dykstra led in the responsive reading, and Rev. Joseph I. Eernisse, gave the invocation. William Miedema rendered a vocal solo. The elders from local churches served the elements. The gracious presence of the Holy Spirit in this service made it a time of earnest thought and spiritual uplift. In the Communion service delegates discovered anew the unity which transcends our differences.

Dr. Daniel A. Poling was the featured speaker over a radio broadcast from the studios of radio station WJEF and was heard over the network of the Columbia Broadcasting System. This program was presided over by Dr. Ernest R. Bryan. Convention musicians, directed by Albert B. McConnell enriched the program with vivid music.

During the Sunday school and morning worship hours, delegates found the churches of their choice. Many convention leaders were guest ministers in the pulpits throughout the area.

As the concluding hour came for this memorable Convention, delegates assembled again in the Civic Auditorium under the chairmanship of Jacob H. Tigelaar.

W E PRESENT again a message in full, that of Dr. Daniel A. Poling, beloved World President of Christian Endeavor, who spoke on "Build With Christ Through World Friendship."

It is a remarkable subject, whatever the message may be, "Build with Christ Through World Friendship."

Ours is one world geographically. It should be a world of friendship. It is not a world of friendship. It is not a world of friendship because ideologically and politically and socially and spiritually it is a sub-divided world, not a world of friendship but a world of animosities that mock. Now, in a small world, this moral and spiritual situation is potential tragedy. What are we going to do about it? What may be done about it?

In 1943 I found myself, ten days before Christmas, half a world way from home, out in China across the hump. I wanted to get home for Christmas, and eventually, I did get home for Christmas. I flew across the continents and high above the sea and reached Philadelphia two days before Christmas. I had spent six days in the journey and only a few hours of that time comparatively in the air, the rest of the time on the ground. I found waiting for me, among other things, a little book printed in Williamsburg, Virginia. That book was the diary of a man who rode 250 years ago from Philadelphia to Williamsburg, about 250 miles, and he spent two weeks in the saddle. He had so many adventures that the story made interesting reading. He spent considerable more time riding a horse between Philadelphia and Williamsburg than I had spent in the air and I really think he had more adventures than I had. The world is changed. It is a small world. A shrunken world that continues to shrink and yet it is a divided, and a sub-divided world. Now what are we going to do about it? Well, there are some things we are doing about it that are inadequate.

Twice within the past eight months, I've heard the Voice of America. I heard it in English out in the Far East or traveling to the Far East and each time I was left strangely depressed. Technically, the Voice was perfect but it lacked something. It lacked the quality

31

of Patrick Henry's, "Give me liberty or give me death." I remember that Felix Morley said in an editorial in *Nation's Business* that what the Voice needed was not more funds but more faith. A friend of mine coming down from Newfoundland heard the Voice and he said, "It left me strangely cold." "I wondered what the little people of the world felt about it," my friend, who was formerly president of Bucknell University, continued. "The speakers were telling of the wonders of America, of the automobiles we had, how many radios we had, and how many deep freezes we had and I knew the Voice was speaking to literally millions of people who could never hope to own an automobile or a deep freeze."

In Manila last November, Dr. Fernando, of the Department of Philosophy of the University of the Philippines, said to me, "Your Voice is mistaken because it shouts democracy to us, and democracy is the unknown word of the unlearned language that we do not care to know because to us out here, democracy has connoted colonialism, economic exploitation, segregation and slavery. It does not mean to us what it undoubtedly means to you. What we need to know is this, may we reasonably hope to have a handful of rice tomorrow?" No, shouting democracy, our democracy to millions over the world will not unite the peoples who are free and who would be free. Where is the opportunity? I think I know, Christian Endeavorers.

"In God We Trust"

There are four words on the coin. You may remember how they got there, of the suggestion that put them there. You may have some conception, at least, of the significance of their presence there. "In God we trust." We've been exporting that dollar. Millions of dollars have been exported by us to the peoples of the earth. Yet, strangely enough, I do not find that we are loved now beyond the love at which we were held before we began to send the dollars overseas. In fact, I've discovered in my journeys that increasingly, our neighbors whom we would have understand us better, understand us less. Perhaps it is because they can not help but envy us. Perhaps it is because even as they received the dollars they got the impression of our power and our might and sometimes our intolerance and our failure to appreciate their problems, too.

I've come back from this most recent mission to Europe with a growing sense of concern, because we fail to get over to the peoples of the earth, the significance of the four words on the coin, "In God we trust." In those words is the opportunity to unite the peoples of the earth who would escape the bondage of Communism. There is opportunity to unite the little people all over the world because there are more than a billion human beings, two hundred million of them behind the iron curtain, who believe in one God. Here is the opportunity for unity. The Buddhists of China and Japan believe in one God; the Moslems of the world believe in one God; the Catholics, Protestants, Jews, inclusively of the orthodox churches of the East, believe in one God. Our own Judaic Christian heritage offers us the opportunity of a platform upon which we may stand to go the length of our common agreement. And if the Voice of America would lift up that, "In God we trust," and would make it increasingly clear, they would find a response from the incurable men and women and little children of the world. You can not destroy that basic thing. In spite of dungeon, fire and sword, in spite of concentration camps and slave centers, men and women believe in one God. And each in his own fashion of these millions, worship one God. That is only the beginning of unity.

Christian Endeavor stands today with Jesus Christ Himself central. Jesus Christ Himself is the only sufficient Saviour. In Him at last there is no east and no west and no north and no south but one vast fellowship of love. I would remind you and you will remember, that in 50 countries of the world, inclusive of the great island groups, there are young people, members of this, the first great ecumenical movement, of all racial strains, who have their unity in Jesus Christ, Son of Man, Son of God, Very God of Very God. Our unity is nowhere else.

United In Christ

This morning at the communion service, which deeply moved me, you were reminded by the one who presided, that we have many patterns for our service of communion. And he called us to a unity beyond all our differences, a unity of faith in that communion service. Of course, unity is not uniformity. You can not have unity unless there are differences and unity always strengthens within those who participate every worthy particular, denominational group, or individual loyalty. You can not have unity unless there is a cause justifying unity. And you can not have unity unless there is one who not only makes it possible, but who also makes it imperative. Our unity is not at last in sacraments, it is not at last in doctrines, it is not at last in creeds, because you see, there are thousands and tens of thousands who do not have a written creed. And there is one great fellowship among us to whom the sacraments are spiritual. Our unity is in Jesus Christ alone, in our acceptance of Him, in our recognition of His deity, in our recognition of those attributions that are His, that make Him all He becomes to us, as Saviour, as Lord, as Redeemer, Redeemer for the individual, Redeemer for the social order, Redeemer for the whole race, Jesus Christ as universal and as personal as He is universal.

Some of you have heard me tell how in World War I, I attended an art exhibition in Paris and how I stood one afternoon before a portrait that was labeled, as I remember it now, "The Galilean," or it may have been "The Mad Dream." It was the production of an artist from North Africa. Unmistakably, the face was the face in the tradition of Jesus. But the Galilean, the Nazarene there, between the thieves, was black as night. And I never thought of Him as black as night. And then He came alive to me as He had never lived for me before and I said, "Of course, here was Jesus. He is like that, every man and every woman claims Him as his own." Mrs. Poling and I were in China for the Christmas holidays in 1935. We sent Christmas cards from Peiping and the baby in the cradle manger was a Chinese baby. Then from Tokyo, we sent New Year's greeting cards. The child pictured on the card was unmistakably a Japanese child. I thought of Jesus as Hoffman's conception: Jesus kneeling by the stone in Gethsemane; Jesus the lad in the temple. And of course, He's like that. Also, He is the Chinese child and the Japanese child, the child of color. Everywhere He is the same—universal. Only one thus, commands the attention of the human race. Perhaps Abraham Lincoln, more than any other, approaches this in quality. Abraham Lincoln is always the rail splitter from Illinois. He is always as American as the frontiers of this continent. Only Jesus is like that. And in Him is unity; in Him is the unity of Christian Endeavor. In Him this afternoon is the opportunity of Christian Endeavorers. Go back to the churches in your communities, go back to your societies, go back to your tasks, whatever they may be believing that in Him is our opportunity to strike a blow not only for freedom, but for the unity of mankind. In the Son of God, whose love passeth knowledge, whose redemption is sufficient, who has the answer, because He is the answer, is our opportunity.

Work In Spain Grows

Only a few weeks ago, I returned from Spain, Italy, France, and England. I spent just two weeks over-seas, and yet in that time I had practically a week in England, I had four days in Barcelona and Madrid. I had a week-end in Rome I had another week-end in Paris. So quickly do we move to and fro, in this small world that I remind you that presently, it will not be necessary for us to leave home, we'll be there before we start We are annihilating space, and yet even more significant than the speed at which I traveled was what I found when I arrived. I found Christian Endeavor in Spain, for instance, where I had not visited in 21 years, organized in 31 societies. And remember, in Spain, Christian Endeavor is practically underground. Young people belong sacrificially and yet twice I met groups as large as 200 each. I've never known more attractive young men and women anywhere and the questions they asked were the questions you've been asking, only they are related to circumstances that you will never know. Here's a Protestant community, a community of our faith with less than twenty thousand in a great land and yet with such power, with such integrity, with such devout purpose . . . Do they give themselves that they grow and beyond all that may be seen in numbers merely, they exert a powerful influence on life in Spain. This same holds for Italy today.

Dr. Bryan ran the roll of countries here a moment ago but there are just two lands which I would take you to this afternoon. The first is Korea. I was in Korea in 1949 in Seoul, then, the land was at peace and the hope of peace was everywhere. Shining faces spoke of the purpose that had become reality—a free land. I met our Christian Endeavorers. I met Kim, of whom Dr. Bryan spoke, the lad from North Korea, who after days of torture had escaped from the Communists after he refused to close the Christian Endeavor office.

Christian Corps In Korea

In Korea last September I looked into the faces of 1,800 volunteers who had just completed their training and within 24 hours were to be inducted into the Army of the Korean

Republic. The corps commander who had enrolled them was Kim Pyung-Sup, chairman of the Korean Christian Endeavor Union, whom I met 15 years ago when he was a lad of 17. Those 1,800 boys stood in a drizzle one Sunday morning at seven o'clock, sang their marching song, "Onward, Christian Soldiers," united in their prayers and listened to my message.

Members of this corps first went into military training with Christian love. They sang in Korean but it was the universal tune and I sang the song that we've sung here and I lifted my hands above my head and clasped them and they lifted their hands toward me. Perhaps you'll be interested in something else that happened that day. The corps commander took a poll. He asked them first, "How many of you drink?" Not a hand went up. He asked the men, "How many of you smoke?" Not a hand went up. They shook their heads. He asked the men, "How many of you swear?" Not a hand went up. They shook their heads. Then he said, "How many of you pray?" They put their two hands up. And I shall see the forest of their hands until I die. Hands uplifted, in 24 hours they'd been activated. We were able to help in a plan by which 800 of them in groups of 100 each went into companies with our American troops. An investigation revealed that the other one thousand were of such quality, nearly all of them having received training in mission schools, that they were made available for special services. And they were scattered throughout the army of South Korea. That was September of last year, young people. You know what has happened since last September—marching to and fro, the burning of the land, that incredible winter, the dying by companies, by battalions, and by regiments. There was a demonstration of the unity that is ours today to which we pledge our lives. That unity in Jesus Christ offers this world redemption from hate, redemption from bitterness, offers this world at last, redemption from iron conflicts, offers the people peace, that is the peace of Christ, that passeth knowledge.

I was in Formosa last November and visited the orphanage in Tycoon, where the journal of which I am editor, takes care of orphan boys and girls. The Communists had closed our orphanages in Fochow and shut down our industrial schools. We opened a great orphanage in Hong Kong to take care of the babies and children from the mainland. It was in Formosa that I heard this story of a lad from the mountains. Formosa is 260 miles long and is an incredibly beautiful and fabulous island. It is 80 miles wide. The population is eight million, about that of Greece. Now two million refugees have been added from the mainland. And that east shore is a rampart, a great range of mountains rising into peaks as high as fourteen thousand feet. A quarter of a million Aborigines live in the mountains. And since the Dutch were there in the 16 hundreds, there had been no regular missionary activities. These Aborigines were head hunters. When the Japanese came nearly 60 years ago and tried to force them to the Shinto Shrine, they refused to go. And they took Japanese heads. Missionary activities down on the plains were conducted on that great church of Canada, the Presbyterian Church of Canada. The mountains had not been penetrated. The Japanese allowed no effort on the part of the great mission Church in the plains to enter the mountains. Then came the war. The Japanese began to take these splendid Aborigines, superior in physical quality. They were drafted into the service. These mountain boys were told that if they were captured by the Americans, first they would be tortured, then they would be killed and then they would be eaten. They particularly did not want to be eaten, so they resolved not to be captured. They fought desperately.

Miracle In Mountains of Formosa

One boy, a remarkable youth, whose father I know now, was sent first to Luzon. He became a sergeant there. Later he fought in New Guinea. He was all but mortally wounded. He was taken prisoner. He tells us now that if he'd been able to, he would have killed the first person in the hospital that came to him. He woke up between sheets. In the hospital he met a man. I do not know him yet. Some day I hope to find him. He met a man who was his physician. A man who was not only a doctor, but a Christian. And this mountain boy, as he looked at that doctor, captured something from him. And presently, he said, "If this is America, and if this is Christianity, I want it. If this is Christianity, I want it." After he recovered sufficiently, he was placed in a prisoner of war camp. That was guarded but it was better than the camps he had known in Luzon. The cease fire was signed on the decks of the Missouri. Eventually, he went home to Formosa, to the high mountains, to his village, to his father's house. There he told his story. The old tribesman, who had 24 heads as his record, was silent. Two days passed. Then he called together the men of tribal importance, and he said to them, "Our son has returned. He's come back telling an unbelievable story. I want him to tell the story to you." So the young man stood and told the story of the Christian doctor of the American hospital, how he had been treated and how he had captured something. He had come back saying, "If this is America and if this is Christianity, I want it." When the boy had finished, the old man stood and said, "If this is Christianity, we do want it. We must find it." There were no missionaries on Formosa, they had not returned. But there were two Bibles in Japanese. They went to work with those Bibles. They taught themselves. The Holy Spirit led them. They did everything they could do. Now the missionaries came back. Senior missionary of the Presbyterian Board came back with his wife. He told the story to me of how he had gone out to the end of the railroad, out to the bridgehead, up on the shoulder of the mountain range, to hold a meeting of Presbyterians. When he got off the train he was surrounded by 700 mountain people. They dress very much as our western Indian dressed. My friend said, "For a moment, I was in mortal terror. Then the old chief stepped up to me and told me the story of his boy. And he said, 'Sir, we've gone as far as we can go. We want to be Christians. If you instruct us, we will become baptized. We would become members of the church.' "

A few months later after they had been instructed, they were baptized. Last November, when I left Formosa, the record stood at 50 churches, 15,000 converted, instructed, baptized members of the church in the mountains. The records are all wrong now. Some of you read my editorial in the last issue of the journal of which I am editor, in which I told of new churches and of how the movement moved down into the south. And listen, these mountain people built their churches without a single dollar from the outside world. Every member of the church is a tither. Men are not allowed to become full members until they've been total abstainers for six months, because liquor has moved in on the mountains. Nothing I've read since the days of the early church could match that. Jesus Christ is adequate. Jesus Christ is the one who is all together lovely and all together powerful. Jesus Christ has the answer because He is the answer. He is the same yesterday, today and forever. If you would have a friendly world then you must bring Him, the great Friend of men and women everywhere. They must have the chance to know Him as you know Him; as Christian Endeavorers know Him through the years; as Christian Endeavorers preached Him everywhere for 70 years.

Stay Through

A good many years ago a young Christian Endeavor secretary came home on call, to meet an emergency. A little son, four years old, needed an operation. He was taken to the clinic. He was in mortal terror. He knew that something impended that was completely new to his desires. And the time came when it was necessary for that father to take the lad in his arms and hold him firmly, pressing him down on the table while they prepared to put the mask upon his little face. Suddenly the boy relaxed. His eyes looked wide into his father's eyes and he said, "Daddy, will you stay through?" And the father said quite casually, glad to be relieved of that increasingly difficult situation, "Yes, son, I'll stay through." They put the mask down on the little boy's face and they gave him the anesthesia. He relaxed completely. The doctor said, "Now you can leave." The father started for the door and something stopped him dead in his tracks. He turned, and he said, "But, doctor, I told him I would stay." The doctor said, "He'll never know, he's asleep now, and when he's awake you'll be here." The father knew better. He said, "No, I'm staying. I promised." And so the father stayed. There came a time when the boy's eyes fluttered open and then dropped shut again. At last they came open and they stayed open. The little fellow focused on his father's face and he fought for words, until he got them. Then he said, "Daddy, did you stay through?" The father is glad to know now that he had the right answer. Sometimes he wonders what might have been had it been the wrong answer. Did you stay through? There have been dedications in this convention, you've heard the call of One who speaks as never a man spake. You said, "yes," to Him, some of you. Others of you have reached a place of high decision in these closing moments. And I'm asking this convention a question. Will you stay through? Will you go back and stay through? Will you return to your own places and stay through? And will you go out then as ministers or as missionaries or as medical missionaries or as educators, out to the far flung battle front of Jesus Christ, the Living Christ, the Prince of Peace, the Great Physician of the body and of the soul. Will you stay for Him? Will the vast majority of you in banks, on farms, in homes as housewives, in business places, as teachers in the schools of the nation, will you as Christians stay through? That is the question. Trusting in the Lord Jesus Christ you may stay through.

Reports were made at this service that 4600 had registered and 2900 delegates had attended, plus visitors.

When the last rich hour of the Convention came and departed, the conviction of all delegates was that they had become energized to go to their separate churches and communities to "Build with Christ." What had once been only a program in black and white, had now evolved into changed lives, enriched thought and determined action on the part of thousands of alert and willing young Christians. The pages of this report cannot present the life-changing decisions, but can only record the fact that this Convention gave young people marvelous opportunities to make decisions "For Christ and the Church," helped older delegates to rededicate themselves and provided a springboard for the program of Christian Endeavor to move into a new era made certain through God's blessings upon a movement exalting His name and work.

Dr. Poling in a typical pose as he spoke at the
closing session of the Convention.

John Delegate's Diary

Monday: Am I glad I came to this Convention! Every moment makes me gladder. Some of those swell-looking pages met me at registration desk and I knew I was going to like this convention from start to finish. There's sure a swell-looking group of girls hanging around all the time.

Tonight at our Regional Quiet Hour I stood next to Mary Lou Sweet. Got to talking with her and found that she knows scads of Endeavorers in our section of the country that I know. I'm taking her to the Regional dinner on Friday. Met Gene Stone and his wife from Columbus headquarters. His million-dollar smile made me feel I had known him for years. His wife sure is nice. Well, we had a hard time getting to bed; everybody of our gang was wound-up. A little night of sleep will set me up for the rest of the week—after that trip and early 4 a.m. leaving.

Tuesday: Didn't expect to like Quiet Hour so much. I had to get up awfully early to be down in time but it was sure worth everything to hear Dr. Prins.

Thought I would take a look at the conference leaders before I chose my conference. They all looked so good that I had a hard time making up my mind. Ernie Marks, who seemed to be in charge of all this, sure had a good lineup of subjects and conference leaders. I finally decided on Clinton Hoggard's conference. Did we have fun building a worship service and one day going to a church to try it out! Listening to Charlie Howe's speech on "Stewardship" in the Assembly convinced me I should join the "Tenth Legion."

Was Dr. Frank F. Warren keen tonight? His outline of "The Master Life" made me resolve to follow the four points to achieve a victorious life with Christ.

Wednesday: Of course the worst day of weather would be the day we would be going to Lake Michigan for our dip at Ottawa Beach. Anyway we had fun in the caravan of cars. Mary Lou got into our car and she is so full of pep that we did not mind the weather.

What a banquet! I never will forget Arch McQuilkin and his lion hunt. Everybody was dressed up in those long dresses and the fellows with their best suits sure did look nice. And such quantities of food. I hope the Convention goes back to Grand Rapids real soon. Albert Arend's "false teeth" as worked by Arch haven't run down yet.

Thursday: All the space in this diary could just about be taken up with the big convention session when Billy Graham spoke. What a night! I got about the last seat left in the top row of the balcony. Lucky that I did not get shoved over into the small auditorium for there was too much going on in the big hall to want to miss any of it. Beverly Shea's solos sort of got under my heart. When Billy Graham stood up he looked like a teen ager, but what a message! Even though I was way up in the balcony I "hit the trail," making a decision for Christ that I will never forget. Prayer with Billy in Room F is one of those high moments I'll never regret.

Friday: Clyde Meadows certainly sparked me to go out to win other youth to Christ when he spoke in the general convention session. After all those quartet numbers from the Pennsylvania delegates and Harold Westerhoff's good humor, everyone was ready to do most anything for Christ and the church. I signed up for my Official Report, not knowing my diary would get into it.

When Norman Paullin told about Naaman and the leper in his sermon tonight I could see how I had been so undecided until last night when I gave my heart to Christ. I just couldn't resist his appeal and Christ's call, and I dedicated myself to full-time Christian service.

Saturday: Here comes the band and the big parade. We marched and marched under the summer heat but it was lots of fun with the streets lined up with Grand Rapids people. The judges and leaders were all on the review-ing stand at Hotel Pantlind and our delegation drew lots of applause.

Was it ever hot! I nearly melted in my outfit, and the red of the cape began to color my shirt. But that didn't make much difference to any of us when we learned hat we had won first prize in the parade.

I liked the Talent program in the evening. It was wonderful to discover what fine talent can be uncovered in our Christian Endeavor groups. I played trumpet solo and it seemed to be much appreciated. Those Grand Rapids musicians that we heard that night and all week certainly are tops.

The last Quiet Hour over at the hotel for our group made me feel almost homesick. I think Mary Lou must have felt the same way for when we decided to go over to the drug store for a soda, she said she just hated to think of the Convention coming to an end. I gave her my address and she is going to write to me as soon as she gets home. We'll keep up the old Convention spirit.

Sunday: It was hard to get up on Sunday morning, but I wouldn't have missed the Communion service for anything. That is one service that always gets under my skin and makes me feel that I ought to be better than I am. We listened to Dr. Poling's broadcast, and it sort of thrilled us to think that this was being heard all over the United States and Canada. That nationwide hookup was certainly a boost for Christian Endeavor.

We went to morning service at the church of our denomination, believing that Christian Endeavorers ought to be loyal to their own denominational group. The pastor's sermon was for youth and certainly stirred us to do more in our church back home.

Our crowd got together at the hotel for dinner Sunday noon. It was our last meal together. We had Rev. and Mrs. Ezekiel Albert, of India as guests. I sat right across from Rev. Mr. Albert and talked to him about India. With Mrs. Albert he leaves August 1 for his homeland. Imagine! It takes six weeks for them to get home, at $600 each.

Mary Lou and I took a walk before the afternoon service and just got into the convention hall as the musical prelude began. I'll remember this service always. It was fun to sit by Mary Lou. Dr. Dan Poling just stirred my soul awake with his concluding message. At the end, all of us had to bow our heads and pray that the hundreds who had found Christ during the Convention would go back to become soul winners and the multitudes of others who re-dedicated themselves would be volunteers for any Christian service that might open in the church or community. When Mary Lou and I joined with the singing of the closing hymn, it seemed that we just couldn't separate. But we know that we have God's work to do and must be builders for Christ and the church wherever we are.

CHAPTER XII

The Junior Convention

SEVEN hundred and eighty-seven Juniors gathered for "Junior Endeavor Day" at the Central Reformed Church. Bus loads and car caravans brought children from Detroit, Kalamazoo, Lansing, Muskegon, Grand Haven, Holland, and several of the smaller cities near Grand Rapids. The morning was a time of fellowship. The walls fairly burst as the children sang favorite choruses. They were entertained by a very clever little Junior reader from Kalamazoo and a man who whistled many beautiful bird calls. Several good movies completed the program.

The order with which the children were marshalled out to lunch in three shifts was wonderful. Everything went smoothly, the children in the sanctuary watching movies and singing choruses, as those in the dining room were eating a good picnic lunch.

Dr. Ernest R. Bryan fascinated the Juniors with the Christian Endeavor chain which Dr. Frences E. Clark wore and which was presented later to Dr. Daniel A. Poling. Now, as president of the International Society, Dr. Bryan possesses it. He suggested that perhaps one of the Juniors present might be the wearer of the president's chain some time in the future.

The Rev. and Mrs. Ezekiel Albert made India live for the boys and girls. They left their address in India with the chairman, suggesting that the Juniors correspond with their children, aged nine and eleven, or with other Indian boys and girls.

The Juniors were the hit of the parade! Preceded by the Junior Christian Endeavor float, wearing Christian Endeavor emblems and carrying pennants and colorful balloons, they marched in orderly columns singing gospel choruses — eight hundred strong.

Tuesday's Junior Workers' Section directed by Viroqua Nodolf stressed these "World Friendship Ideas:"

1. Interest children in persons rather than causes.

2. Create interest, understanding, and the desire to share with other people.

3. Give to missions, but give for a specific project. Educate the boys and girls to give regularly, proportionately, and with a definite purpose.

4. Introduce boys and girls to people who have given their lives to Christian service. Help them to know missionaries as real people who have a concern for all God's children.

5. Challenge Junior boys and girls to think about their life work. Help them to think in terms of Christian Service.

Wednesday's Workshop treated music, worship and audio-visual resources. Miss Nodolf differentiated between four kinds of religious songs and their use with children: the hymn, the gospel song, the fellowship chorus and the devotional chorus. She urged care that all music used be within the religious concept of the child, and that we take *good music* and by education make it popular with the children.

Mrs. Marian Hoopes led the Worship Workshop presenting a visual program which she had prepared for Mother's Day use in Pennsylvania. The lovely kodachrome slides, most of them actual photos of real people, were supplemented by explanatory records and coordinated music. The program closed with the singing of the hymn "When Little Children Pray" which can be found in "Christian Endeavor Songs," obtainable through the International Society.

Thursday's conference leader, Miss Margaret Paugh, of the Junior Work Committee stressed the importance of the Junior Christian Endeavor Covenant as a basis of membership in the society—but gave this caution. The child and parents must thoroughly understand the pledge, and the child must have help in keeping it.

The general subject for Friday was "Recreation for Juniors." The period was turned from a formal session to an exceedingly informal one. The adult leaders became "Juniors" for a time and participated beautifully in the songs and games which were presented.

Dr. and Mrs. Gene Stone and Family.

CHAPTER XIII

When Everybody Shared

THE daily meeting of 50 leaders for mental and spiritual refreshment was in fact a most significant occasion. Seated at tables in groups of eight, the chairman of the educational conferences, Ernest S. Marks and conference leaders and guest speakers had unusual opportunities to share their ideas regarding the work of the day and the significance of the previous day's session.

Ernest S. Marks

The group overflowed with valuable suggestions to make the Convention features even more significant. Each morning Mr. Marks dealt with the theme of the forum series. Dr. Stone, Dr. Poling and others made significant contributions. The group was sent on to the Quiet Hour and the morning discussion periods by a brief inspirational message each morning given by Dr. Clyde W. Meadows.

The educational conferences of the Grand Rapids Convention were ranged in two age group divisions as follows: (1) for young people 18 years of age and upwards; (2) for high school ages under 18. There were two periods held daily. During the first period practical implications of the theme for the day were discussed. During the second period conferences dealing with Christian Endeavor principles and methods were held.

All delegates were enrolled in a given conference group in each of the two periods. In these conferences young persons were directed by capable leaders to express their points of view and to make concrete suggestions for the solution of youth problems and the enrichment of youth work in the church. The democratic procedures permitted free-for-all discussion and made this "School" of the Convention among the most helpful features of the Convention. Subjects for the days were as follows:

Tuesday: "Build with Christ"

Wednesday: "Build with Christ—through Personal Dedication"

Thursday: "Build with Christ—through Church Loyalty"

Friday: "Build with Christ—through Christian Citizenship"

Saturday: "Build with Christ—through World Friendship"

Leaders were as follows: Rev. Clair E. Beatty, Rev. Henry Bast, Rev. Elwood Dunn, Mrs. Alice Griffin, Rev. J. Clinton Hoggard, Rev. John F. Little, Miss Christina E. MacAskill, Paul F. Hurley, Dr. R. W. Rash, Rev. J. Wesley Siebert, Rev. Donald D. Abbey, Rev. Brenton J. K. Arthur, Rev. George C. Douma, Rev. Earle W. Gates, Warren G. Hoopes, and Rev. R. Ward Williams.

Conferences on Principles and Methods of Youth Work with their leaders were as follows:

Christian Endeavor Essentials, Rev. Clair E. Beatty; Building the Total Program of the Society, Miss Christina E. MacAskill; Enriching Worship in the Society, Rev. J. Clinton Hoggard; Building Your Society Membership, Paul F. Hurley; Improving Society Devotional Meetings, Rev. Elwood Dunn; Organization and Functions of a Christian Endeavor Society, Rev. J. Wesley Siebert; World Outreach for the Society, Rev. John F. Little; Publicity That Gets Results, Galen Colclesser; Christian Endeavor Essentials, Charles O. Heyward; Building the Total Program of the Society, Mrs. Alice Griffin; Enriching Worship in the Society, Rev. George C. Douma; Building Your Society Membership, Rev. Donald D. Abbey; Improving Society Devotional Meetings, Warren G. Hoopes; Publicity That Gets Results, Rev. Wellington W. Whittlesey; Winning Youth to Christ, Rev. Earle W. Gates; Planning Recreation Activities, Rev. Brenton J. K. Arthur.

Attention was given to pastors and counselors of youth with these leaders presenting helpful materials: Rev. R. Ward Williams, Dr. R. W. Rash, and Arch J. McQuilkin.

The Union Leaders' Section was led by Ernest S. Marks, with Phil C. Reed, chairman.

Selected subjects for intensive study by older young people and leaders of youth were as follows:

Fellowship of Prayer, Mrs. Daniel A. Poling, leader; Evangelism, Dr. Elmer Becker; Life Work, Dr. Frank F. Warren; How to Study the Bible, Dr. Norman W. Paullin; Gettings Results from Alcohol Education, Rev. Henry C. Jacobs; Christian Citizenship, Dr. Ernest R. Bryan; Missionary, Rev. and Mrs. Ezekiel F. Albert; Audio-Visual, Lester Martin.

A wealth of material came out of these periods. The gist of these successful hours spent together by hundreds of Endeavorers and leaders must be compressed into a few pages—but we believe the material is of profit for reading and study. The conference leaders gladly give credit to delegates who shared in these sessions for adding many of the comments and raising numerous questions that increased and deepened the total educational value of the group gatherings.

Build with Christ

THE day by day treatment of the Convention theme as discussed the first hour of the Educational Conferences generally followed this pattern as set down by *Rev. Henry Bast's* group:

I—Build with Christ
    A—What does Christ want us to build?
        1. The Kingdom of God
          a—Christ-like Lives
          b—Christian Homes
          c—Spiritual Church
    B—What is our relationship to Christ in this Kingdom?
        1. He is our Lord and Savior
          a—We owe Him our absolute Authority
          b—He is the Son of God

II—Build with Christ through personal dedication
    A—What is personal dedication?
        1. Giving ourselves to Christ in complete surrender

a—Repentance from sin (Mark 1:4, Matt. 3:2, Luke 13:3)
b—Faith (knowledge and trust) (John 3:16, Acts 16:31, Romans 10:9, 10)
2. Growing in knowledge and in the Christian life (Col. 1:6)
3. Giving of our service in furthering His Kingdom

III—Build with Christ through Church Loyalty
A—We must have a knowledge of what the Church is
1. It is the House of God, where His Word is preached
2. It is a Fellowship of believers
3. It is the Body of Christ's redeemed
B—What is the Nature of the Church?
1. Catholic
a—It has historical, visible continuity
2. Protestant
a—Form (Visible)
1) Where Word of God is truly preached
2) Where Sacraments are rightly administered
b—Essence (Invisible)

IV—Build with Christ through Christian Citizenship
A—Our responsibility (1 Peter 2:13, Romans 13:1)
B—Foundation of Christian Citizenship
1. Must be born again; changed from the desire to hate to the desire to love.
2. Principle of authority is necessary
a—Fifth Commandment—"Honor thy father and thy mother" (Cannot bring a Youth Program into the church successfully unless we have this principle of authority in the home first of all.)

To this list *Rev. J. W. Siebert's* group adds:

"The person who knows Christ will:

a. Help support the young people's program

b. Tell others about Him

c. Be at church instead of the many other places that claim the time of young people

d. Try to fulfill His purposes instead of their own

e. Strive to build His kingdom with love."

This group also suggests that to "Build with Christ—Through World Friendship," Christian Endeavor

a. Will use missionary books and programs of denomination

b. Will encourage correspondence with "foreign" pen pals

c. Will send food and clothing to needy countries (CARE, etc.)

d. Will sponsor D.P.s in immigration

e. Will study the United Nations Organization

f. Will practice charity toward all races.

The *Rev. Mrs. Alice A. Griffin's* group reviewed Christian Endeavor's covenant and said that Christian Endeavorers have a loyalty first to Christ's church and then to those in governmental position who will "Build With Christ" great Christian nations.

Warren G. Hoopes' sectional conference held that "God is the Architect, the Bible has building plans and we are the builders."

Christina E. MacAskill's group says: "Before we can build with Christ we must know Him as the one and only sure Foundation for the structure which we would erect. As we build we grow for the verb 'build' means progress. In this task we are not working alone. 'With' suggests companionship in the task. It is a companionship with Christ who will see us through to final success."

Rev. J. Clinton Hoggard's group holds that "after one comes to know Christ and willingly commits his life to serving Christ, he must give of himself and his time and his possessions freely to Christ without reservation.

"Therefore a full complete personal dedication of one's life to Jesus Christ and His teachings causes him to grow loyal to the church, become a citizen of the kingdom of God by doing God's will and bearing witness for Christ at home and abroad. These practices make a person know that racial barriers, economic differences and social-denominational divisions are all wiped out because of the oneness in his soul which is evidence of God's grace working through man by his faith in Jesus Christ, the Master-builder."

Paul Hurley's group stimulatingly says: "World friendship must begin at home. It is senseless to think that we can live in a world peaceably when we cannot live in a neighborhood peaceably. Intolerance must be abolished and a true understanding, love and appreciation of all people must be built up within our hearts and minds."

Rev. John Little challenged his group with this statement: "Don't waver in your conviction of Christ."

Rev. Brenton J. K. Arthur's group held that to Build with Christ first requires a personal knowledge and acceptance of Him as a Person and as a personal Saviour, coupled with a wholehearted acceptance of His program and surrender to Him.

Rev. Henry Bast's discussion group held that Christian Endeavor must train all Christians to THINK in world terms. It must produce Christian statesmen who think in terms of righteousness and God.

Rev. Earle W. Gates' group asked: "What are we going to build?" and answered: (1) new habits; (2) new program; (3) loyalty. Another question was: "How am I going to build?" Members replied: (1) through life planning; (2) reading the Bible; (3) counseling with those who know.

Rev. Clair E. Beatty's group concluded: "If this convention is a success, it will be as individuals return to homes, societies, churches, and communities to 'Build with Christ' by proving the effectiveness of their personal dedication to Him."

Rev. Don Abbey's group endeavored to secure a definition of "loyalty" and held that "loyalty is being true to one's God, highest beliefs and deepest friendships."

Rev. George C. Douma's conference discussion group held that "To build with Christ surrender to Christ is a must." In discussing World Friendship "Christianity relies on the power of God and not on the energies of men. This is a great age of opportunity for Christian missions."

Rev. R. Ward Williams group endeavored to secure Scripture passages which reveal loyalty on its highest levels.

Counselor's Section

"THE spirit of youth is unconsciously searching for that which is alive and exciting," young people's age-group pastors and counselors concluded in *Dr. R. W. Rash's* conferences. "Christian Endeavor will pulsate with life when leaders emphasize the historical background and the cardinal principles of the movement as founded by Dr. Francis E. Clark.

"Christian Endeavor is evangelistic," the group continued. "The first principle is confession of Christ—the fundamental beginning. Then follows service for Christ—necessary corollary; loyalty to Christ's church, the profound obligation; fellowship with Christ's people, the essential unity."

Counselors of young adult groups in *Rev. R. Ward Williams'* Conference agreed that "much experimentation needs to be done in this age group. It was firmly felt that a young adult group should not be organized just for a social function but that the group should make a definite contribution to the spiritual life and work of the church.

"Before starting a group the pastor should select carefully a few key people to go over church lists and look for all possibilities for membership. The group may make up only a loose organization. Too many officers are not needed. Map out a program for opening and successive nights. Then plan a visitation of the community inviting young adults to attend."

Arch J. McQuilkin's group of Junior High and Senior High Counselors, held that "wise counselors will be Christian through and through and as the disciples, we will be a believer, a follower, a student, a pupil, a learner. The counselor must not forget that he is a human being and must act the part by getting along with people and by learning to love them.

"Our manner of reaching the young people is through the Sunday evening meetings or other opportune times. We must not lead but give the young people advice and let them have charge of their meetings, remembering to include devotions, singing, prayer, helpful topics, Bible quizzes, discussion."

Christian Endeavor Union leaders met under the direction of *Mr. Ernest S. Marks.* They summarized their task thus:

"Christian Endeavor in every sense uses the universal principles and ideals of the Christian cause. The Christian Endeavor Union aims to '   emphasize the spiritual and leadership training values of Christian Endeavor for all young people, to this end stimulating interest in societies of Christian Endeavor, promoting their efficiency as factors in Christian life and church work by bringing them into closer relationship with one another, and making it possible for them to work together in common enterprises'."

Principles and Methods of Youth Work

"No amount of consecration can make up for wastefulness of unplanned work; no worthwhile programs ever 'just happen'," was the conclusion of *Mrs. Alice Griffin's* Conference group on "Building the Total Program of the Society."

"Successful program-building must take into account these basic principles:

1. The needs and interests of the group.
2. Objectives of the "Vital Program for Youth," denominational and local church objectives.
3. Must center in persons.
4. Should be planned locally and by youth with adult counsel.
5. As an integral part of the total youth program of the church.
6. Vital relationship to the program of the denomination and include participation in the program of International Christian Endeavor Union, State and Local Unions.
7. Be planned well in advance—outlined for a full year and details lifted up monthly or quarterly.

Six basic faults of meetings were listed by *Rev. Elwood Dunn's* group as delegates considered "Better Devotional Meetings." They are: (1) Too monotonous; (2) Lack of preparation—a. by leader; b. by group; (3) Lack of spiritual depth; (4) Inadequate use of material; (5) Lack of use of originality; (6) Leadership problems.

Essentials of a good meeting were outlined thus by *Warren G. Hoopes'* group in "Improving Society Devotional Meetings" · (1) Good topic; (2) Well planned program; (3) Definite purpose; (4) Fitting Service of Worship; (5) Reverence; (6) Cooperation of members; (7) Plenty of prayer; (8) Attractive meeting place; (9) Variety; (10) Good group singing; (11) Individual participation.

Paul F. Hurley's group on "Building Your Society Membership" held that the Membership (Lookout) Committee not only is responsible for the gaining of new members but must be concerned with the holding of the present members. In line with these functions, it is imperative that there be close cooperation between Membership Committee and the various other divisions in the group organization.

"We must have a definite and clear plan if we are to succeed in securing new members. The 3-4-1 plan, a method whereby a committee of three members is responsible for one prospective-named member, is ofttimes successful.

"Above all, each member of the Membership Committee must have a genuine concern for people—'A passion for the work.' A praying Membership Committee may be the difference in many societies between success and failure."

Galen Colclesser's group on "Publicity That Gets Results" discussed the important problems in Christian Endeavor publicity: Understanding, community spirit, good will, ways of informing the public of Christian Endeavor programs, personalities, spiritual growth, leadership training possibilities, personal preparation, how to get the people to attend, a soul-winning campaign, advertising and visiting.

On the same subject *Rev. W. W. Whittlesey's* conference group made these pointed suggestions: (1) State only facts. (2) Tell the story briefly, then stop. (3) Make the story clear and accurate. (4) Be careful about paragraphing, punctuating, names, titles and dates. (5) Avoid abbreviations, slang and adjectives. (6) Clean, double-spaced and neat paper should be submitted.

Rev. Brenton J. K. Arthur's group on "Planning Recreation Activities" observed that a good recreation leader should have three qualifications: (1) He must understand youth and be youthful in mind. (2) He must know how to play, and be a leader in the art of playing; and (3) He must be a Christian in order to know pleasure and playing at its best.

"The Recreation Committee, being but one committee of the society, must not feel that it is the only, or even the most important committee in the society; but must work in co-operation and conjunction with other committees, not only in timing, but also in planning and program; aiming to make the social life of the society complement the entire program."

In considering the "World Outreach for the Society," *Rev. John F. Little's* group suggested:

"Encourage C.E. societies to invite foreign students to their meetings, that they might become indoctrinated in the principles of Endeavor work.

"Encourage missionaries to organize C.E. societies on foreign fields. In these days of uncertainty, chaos, and confusion, Christian Endeavorers must work as never before to Build with Christ through their societies here and abroad.

"Encourage State Unions to further C.E. by training native Endeavorers for foreign work. (Pennsylvania pays for a native Field Secretary in India.)"

Chief emphases of *Charles O. Heyward's* group in "Christian Endeavor Essentials" were:

"The spiritual and moral needs of young people today and how Christian Endeavor can meet them; the importance of the individual young person in the spiritual program of the society; the qualifications of leaders and of those who conduct the weekly meetings; reviving the challenge of the Quiet Hour, Tenth Legion and Life Work Recruits; the society in the wider fellowship of other Christians and of the CE Union; the constant need of prayer, and the prime purpose of helping young people to know Christ and to want to serve Him and the church."

Rev. Henry C. Jacob's Conference group on "Getting Results from Alcohol Education" held that

"In America the alcohol problem has been assuming tremendous proportions with 60,000,000 people drinking alcoholic beverages, with 4,000,000 belonging to the early alcoholics or problem drinkers and 900,000 chronic alcoholics, with an average of $60 being spent by every man, woman and child, with television and radio and newspaper and magazine advertising constantly promoting sales, with 428,000 outlets compared with 170,000 saloons in bygone days; with 16,000,000 women drinking and a million or more new drinkers added every year. All this is adding to the growing gravity of the situation until thousands are asking, where will it end, what will it lead to?

"Young people today are challenged also because there is such a vast fund of new scientific information on what Alcohol is and does. Containing heat energy but not vitamins, steady drinkers have resistance lowered against such diseases as pellegra and Berri-berri, health authorities tell us it is being used for medicine from 70-80% less than formerly, science has no way of telling who when he starts to drink may become an Alcoholic, the higher functions of the brain, conscience, judgment, self control and the capacity for self-criticism are affected."

Rev. Earle W. Gates' group on "Winning Youth to Christ" held that "there is a great need for winning others to Christ in this world and it is up to us Christians to do it. The life we live, and our actions and words can win others every day. God will always stand by us if we are willing and faithful enough to do our part."

Christina E. MacAskill's conference on "Planning the Total Program of the Society," held that "a Christian Endeavor Society should be so built that every need and interest of the members receive proper emphasis. Leaders must know the fundamental principles of the organization and plan that these emphases become a vital part of every activity. Christian Endeavor is a training school which utilizes the "learn by doing" technique. Each member should receive a definite assignment in order that he may share in the work of the society and by so doing receive valuable training for kingdom service. The best programs result from a careful study of Christian Endeavor, denominational and local church plans and materials for young people."

Rev. Don Abbey's group discussion on "Building Your Society Membership" discussed first how to retain the loyalty of present members, then how to win old members back, and finally the means of attracting new members. Attractive programs, personal interest, Sunday school roll check-up, Friendship parties, were a few of the means suggested.

Special Conference Section

For older young people and leaders of youth specialized subjects were explored. *Dr. Elmer Becker's* group on "Evangelism" held that folks are not so much "gospel hardened" as "method hardened." They quoted Dr. Poling: "We can have no new world without new world builders" and then said: "We can has no new world builders without new hearts." One's personal testimony can be expressed in two means—by our walk and our talk.

An interesting project was undertaken by several members of the group. This project was to discover the means by which Christians were led to become a Christian. In reporting on this project it was interesting to note the various manners in which Christians had accepted Jesus Christ as their Lord and Saviour. Several stated it was through revival meetings, other means were through friends, regular church services, ministers, mothers, Christian Endeavor, reading the Bible and camp affiliations.

Methods of evangelism were considered including surveys, evangelistic missions to youth, Sunday school, Decision Days, revivals, visitation campaigns, Sunday services and C. E. meetings. The Christian Endeavor plan of Youth Evangelism as suggested in the little book, "Acquainting Youth with Christ," by Leslie was mentioned as an excellent guide for planning an evangelistic campaign among the youth of the church. Young people who are earnest Christians can better work with young people who are non-Christians in such a youth-winning campaign.

Dr. Frank Warren's group in Life Work said the "Will of God" may be outlined thus:

Jesus said "My will is to do the will of Him who sent me." He that doeth the will of God abideth forever.

(1) *Spacious*: God pushes out the horizons of life. Interests become greater constantly.

(2) *Specific*: God takes into mind every detail of our lives. He is the most methodical being the world has ever known.

(3) *Supreme*: His will has to be supreme seven days of the week. Takes in your friendships, your work and your whole living.

(4) *Safe*: The will of God is safe. Life is not duration, but rather— donation. If you are doing God's will, you are in the safest place of the world. You have no right to live carelessly.

Knowing God's plan may be discovered thus: (1) Through prayer— Seek daily communion; (2) Through Scriptures—Bible is a guide to everyday living; (3) Through providential circumstances—Workable tests: a. Is this the Lord's work? b. Am I the man to do it? c. Is this the way it should be done? d. Is the time ripe for doing it?

Dr. Norman W. Paullin's conference delved into "How to Study the Bible." These five plans were offered:

(1) The Bible as a complete book. This volume was written by forty writers over a period of 1500 years, yet has a central character and one theme. The best way to view a city is by airplane. We cannot know the Bible until we have given it a chance.

(2) Each Book as a unit of the whole. This seems like a very natural method. Study the Book historically. (a) Know the writer. (b) Know the people to whom he spoke or wrote. (c) Know the conditions religiously and socially. (d) Outline the Book by means of the main thoughts.

(3) Subject study and character study. (a) Know the great doctrines of our faith by following their unfolding through the 66 books. The subjects are endless. (b) Every kind of character known to man is found in the Bible. Biography is always interesting. (c) In this method you need a good concordance.

(4) Chapter Study. Study at least one chapter of God's Word each day. Find the "gold nuggets."

(5) Word Study. Obtain from the best means at your disposal the *strict, exact* and full meaning of words and names employed by the sacred writers.

The Bible is more than history, biography, ethics, or literature. It is the *Book of Life.*

"India today is 'a field white unto the harvest,'" said *Rev. and Mrs Ezekiel Albert* in the missionary conference.

Missionaries from other countries are both necessary and welcome when they bring the Christian spirit which enables them to work with and under the direction of Indian Christian leaders. Most urgent is the development of nationals to take the Christian message to their own people.

Christian medical missionaries and lay health service workers are needed and have here a great opportunity for Christian witness.

The demand for education is such that teachers are working double shifts. Only 20% of people can read and write. There is no opportunity for free education in India. A student can be supported in India for five American dollars per month, and may receive Christian training in hostels connected with the schools. It is only through reducing the illiteracy of India we can hope to win them to Christ.

Timely films were shown in the group on "Audio Visual Aids" directed by *Lester Martin.* Demonstration of projectors and discussion centered on techniques. Suggestions given in class as helps in visual aids included:

A. Keep church well lit up so that they may be noticed easily at a distance.

B. More money should be spent for correct and Christian advertising.

C. Plan program in advance, in other words, have equipment set up and ready to run when you are showing films.

D. Have equipment that is light and easy to handle so that it may be used for shut-ins as well as groups, conferences and respective church meetings.

E. Take tape recordings that may be used for future programs, teas or social gatherings.

F. Light projectors used for a means of memorizing.

G. Use of hands over the lens for effective fade-in's and out's of pictures.

The conference in Christian Citizenship under the direction of *Dr. Ernest R. Bryan,* was of a workshop type in which a different "Citizen of the Day" brought first hand helps and answers to questions out of their own experience.

Norman Klauder, businessman of Philadelphia, said: "A true Christian is always a good citizen but a good citizen is not necessarily a Christian."

Dr. Daniel A. Poling, head of All-American Conference to Combat Communism and candidate for mayor of Philadelphia, held:

"Communism tries to split our thinking by racial prejudice. Democracy is not crystalized and must continue to go forward. The majority must see that the minority has its rights   The answer to Communism is Christian lives wholly consecrated and dedicated to Christ in every phase of life at all times."

Albert Arend, businessman of Spokane, Washington, believed that "What happens to us in life is not as important as our attitudes concerning hese."

Rev. Charles E. F. Howe, Director of ISCE's new Citizenship Department, stated: "We are officers in the army of the Lord with a commission to Build With Christ. The enemy is well entrenched and we must know how to combat him. *Preparation*: Share the Word and spread it. *Re-enforcement*: The family altar makes Christian homes which make Christian communities.

Dr. Frank F. Warren, president of Whitworth College, Spokane, Wash., challenged: "Christian youth must go into politics as well as full time Christian service. A new department of Foreign Service is being set up at Whitworth with this thought in mind. Don't take just any job, don't be just a bread-winner, BE A TRAIL-BLAZER!!"

Mrs. Daniel A. Poling's conference on "Fellowship of Prayer" went deeply into the techniques and values of prayer. "The ultimate solution to all our problems is found in practicing the presence of God," averred the participants. "Prayer is cooperation with God. Each person influences an average of 52 people (according to statistics). If every Christian would influence 52 others for Christ, we could save the world . . . and we should start working at it."

CHAPTER XIV

Youth Assembly Voices
Youth's Convictions

AN important group in the total convention was the Youth Assembly of the International Society of Christian Endeavor. This Assembly was established only a few bienniums ago to insure the voice of youth being heard in the activities and program of the parent organization. Harold Davidson, Columbus, Ohio, the Assembly president, directed the Assembly sessions and represented this group on the Board of Trustees.

Harold Davidson

International Society leaders met with the Assembly each day. On Tuesday Dr. Clyde W. Meadows spoke on the Convention's theme: "Build with Christ," stressing four main points: Personal Dedication, Church Loyalty, Christian Citizenship, and World Fellowship. Wednesday the Assembly heard President Ernest R. Bryan of the International Society and President Daniel A. Poling of the World's Union. Thursday, Rev. Charles Howe presented Christian Citizenship and Stewardship and Dr. Gene Stone told of the educational work and publications of the Society. Friday, Ernest Marks and Mac Cochran led discussions on the proposed United Strategy.

Discussions centered on the five principal questions the International Society of Christian Endeavor desired discussed by the Youth Assembly:

1—What should be the duties of the Associate President of the I.S.C.E.? Should he be chosen by the Board of Trustees or by recommendation by the Youth Assembly?

2—Should International Trustees named by the Youth Assembly meet by themselves to formulate recommendations before they are presented to the Board of Trustees as a whole?

3—Should Youth Assembly take up specific projects, missionary programs connected with work of the World Christian Endeavor Union?

4—Should we have a representative in Honolulu at the World Union meeting July 26-30, 1952? If so, what should the responsibilities of this delegation be?

5—What part can the Youth Assembly play in the new crusade for Christian Citizenship and the continuing Evangelistic Missions to Youth.

Recommendation was made to the Board of Trustees that the plan of Youth Assembly function in State Unions and that the plan of organization for the State Union be adopted.

It was recommended that one delegate go to the Honolulu Convention to represent the Youth Assembly.

A Get-Acquainted Party was held Thursday.

These officers were named, all of whom become members of the Board of Trustees of the International Society:

Chairman—Richard Pruiksma, Clifton, New Jersey.

Vice Chairman—Jack Graf, Mercedes, Texas.

Secretary—Peggy Mangum, Fairfield, Alabama.

Rep. to Program Council—Marjorie Stiggers, Chicago, Ill.

Rep. to Program Council—Harold E. Davidson, Columbus, Ohio.

Alternate to Program Council—Eunice Nelson, Washington, D. C.

Evangelistic Mission to Youth—Vernon Hoffman, Kalamazoo, Michigan.

Trustees at Large—Vicky Fair, Denver, Colorado; Florence Wright, Buechel, Kentucky; Bob McQuilkin, Stratford, Pa.

These resolutions as adopted by the Youth Assembly have wider import:

Resolutions concerning Youth Assembly delegates.

Be it resolved that the trustees be the ad-interim body for the Youth Assembly at all stated meetings.

Be it resolved that the Youth Assembly hereby express its appreciation to the staff of the ISCE for the splendid cooperation which was evident and the fine way in which they provided us with our splendid program.

Resolutions of the Youth Assembly of ISCE
Be it resolved that

The trustees of the Youth Assembly meet concurrently with the program committee and the executive's conference.

The *Christian Endeavor World* carry periodical articles written by members of the Youth Assembly.

The Youth Assembly put their full support behind the "Build With Christ" through Christian Citizenship Crusade.

The Youth Assembly support the Evangelistic Missions to Youth and the 70th Anniversary Advance.

The International Society encourage the several states to establish Youth Assemblies.

The International Society encourage the several states to bring up to date the mailing lists of individual societies and the members of Youth Assembly shall stand ready to assist in this program.

The functions and duties of the Youth Assembly as established by the Board of Trustees be defined more clearly.

The Youth Assembly be represented at all conferences, conventions, committees, and/or other interdenominational programs where Christian Endeavor is invited or represented.

Our Leaders for the New Biennium

One of the important actions of the Board of Trustees was the naming of new leaders to direct the work of the International Society of Christian Endeavor and the Corporation for the next two years. Those selected are:

INTERNATIONAL SOCIETY OF CHRISTIAN ENDEAVOR

Officers

Dr. Ernest R. Bryan _____President
LaVerne H. Boss _____Associate President
Albert Arend _____Vice-President
B. McClain Cochran _____Vice-President
Rev. J. Clinton Hoggard _____Vice-President
Mrs. Joseph Holton Jones _____Vice-President
Dr. Clyde W. Meadows _____Vice-President
Dr. Gene Stone _____Clerk and General Secretary
Rev. Charles E. F. Howe _____Associate General Secretary
Harold E. Westerhoff _____Administrative Secretary
Rev. Charles E. F. Howe _____Treasurer
William J. von Minden _____Auditor

Vice-Presidents in Charge of Regions

Herman Decker _____North Atlantic
J. Allen Tucker _____Middle Atlantic
Phyllis G. Brown _____Southern
Julian Moran _____Great Lakes
Arloa Muilenburg _____Central
Dr. J. Wilson Byers _____Rocky Mountain
J. C. Estes _____South Western
Mrs. Reba C. Rickman _____Pacific
Rev. J. Wesley Siebert _____Dominion of Canada

Members of The Executive Committee

Albert Arend	Miss Christina MacAskill
Allan J. Blair	H. Lewis Mathewson
LaVerne H. Boss	Dr. Clyde W. Meadows
Dr. Ernest R. Bryan	Frederick L. Mintel
Rev. Lester H. Case	Julian Moran
B. McClain Cochran	Dr. Reuben H. Mueller
Dr. Harold M. Dudley	Dr. Daniel A. Poling
Rev. Earle W. Gates	Richard Pruiksma
Rev. J. Clinton Hoggard	Merritt L. Smith
Norman Klauder	Rev. J. Wesley Siebert

Carroll M. Wright

Board of Trustees
Trustees Representing the Evangelical Denominations

African Methodist Episcopal Church _____Dr. C. W. Abington
                                                        Dr. U. S. Robinson
African Methodist Episcopal Zion Church _____Dr. James W. Eichelberger
                                                        Dr. William J. Walls
Church of God _____Adam W. Miller
Churches of God (General Eldership) _____V. O. Barnhart
Church of the Nazarene _____C. Edwin Harwood
                                                        Mendell L. Taylor
Congregational-Christian Churches _____James A. G. Moore
                                                        Rev. Carl A. Hansen
                                                        George A. Stickney

James G. Laing
Guy P. Leavitt
Christina E. MacAskill
Ernest S. Marks
H. Lewis Mathewson
Arch J. McQuilkin
Dr. Clyde W. Meadows
Luther R. Medlin
Frederick L. Mintel
Rev. Jerry Moore
Julian Moran
Dr. S. S. Morris
Dr. Reuben H. Mueller
Arloa Muilenburg
Viroqua Nodolf
Elmer Olson
Fred D. Parr
Dr. Daniel A. Poling

Fred B. Porter
Phil C. Reed
Rev. Thomas Rennie
Mrs. Reba C. Rickman
Fred R. Roy
Rev. J. Wesley Siebert
Merritt L. Smith
Rev. George R. Sweet
Dr. George Oliver Taylor
Jacob H. Tigelaar
J. Allen Tucker
William J. von Minden
Frederick A. Wallis
Dr. Frank F. Warren
Frank P. Wilson
Rev. William S. Wise
Margaret Wood
Carroll M. Wright

Presidents and Employed General, Executive, and/or Field Secretary of State, Provincial, and Territorial Christian Endeavor Unions

ALABAMA—David L. Boozer (P)
CALIFORNIA—Milo E. Hall (P)
—Rev. Jerry Yerian (FS)
COLORADO—Dr. J. Wilson Byers (P)
CONNECTICUT—Althea F. Stearns (P)
DELAWARE—Stanley J. Kersey (P)
DEL., D. C., & MD.—
Charles O. Heyward (FS)
DIST. OF COL.—Carl Powell (P)
GOLDEN RULE—Mrs. Rosa Lee Jones (P)
—Phil C. Reed (FS)
IDAHO—Marvin D. Linscheid (P)
ILLINOIS—Henry J. Skinner (P)
—Rev. Wellington W. Whittlesey (FS)
INDIANA—Ward Houser (P)
IOWA—Wilma Maassen (P)
KANSAS—Arthur W. Preston (P)
KENTUCKY—Rev. Ralph D. McLean (P)
MARYLAND—Edward T. Gilliss (P)
MASSACHUSETTS—
Kenneth A. MacRae (P)
—Christina MacAskill (ES)
MICHIGAN—LaVerne H. Boss (P)
—Rev. Elwood Dunn (GS)
MINNESOTA—Rev. Parks T. Hunt (P)
MISSOURI—Paul Gillam (P)
NEBRASKA—Mrs. Vivian J. Ingraham (P)
NEW JERSEY—Harold E. Westerhoff (P)
—Frederick L. Mintel (ES)
NEW YORK—Russell S. Gowdey (P)
—Rev. Walter C. Schaeffer (GS)
NORTH CAROLINA—Mrs. Ruth Lee (P)
—Tracey Miller (GS)
OHIO—Robert S. Hildreth
—Rev. Brenton J. K. Arthur (ES)
OREGON—Donna Lee Plymale (P)
—Dorothy Howes (ES)
PENNSYLVANIA—Paul F. Hurley (P)
—Warren G. Hoopes (GS)

TENNESSEE—Mary Fisher (P)
TEXAS—Patsy Nixon (P)
UTAH—Lawrence Lister (P)
VIRGINIA—Cecil A. Slaughter (P)
WASHINGTON—Jacqueline Slining (P)
WEST VIRGINIA—Mrs. Norval Newlon (P)
WISCONSIN—Wyman J. Kastein (P)
CANADA, ONT.—Ray Zimmerman (P)
CANADA, QUE.—H. P. B. Carter (P)
CANADA—Rev. J. Wesley Siebert (P)
HAWAII—Walter Nomura (P)
—Harold C. Smith (FS)
HAWAII (CE Ass'n)—
Rev. Edward Kahale (P)

Dr. Poling installs the officers for the new biennium.

CHAPTER XV

We Hereby Resolve

Committee on Resolutions

Our Seventieth Anniversary

Whereas the 41st International Convention of Christian Endeavor, meeting in Grand Rapids, Michigan, July 9-15, on the occasion of the 70th anniversary of the movement's foundation, desires to place in the records of its proceedings its thankfulness to Almighty God for the blessings of these seven decades.

We register our belief that the movement was born in the mind and heart of God to fill a need in the life of the church in its service to youth. We are grateful that the inspired objective and purpose of the organization has remained unchanged, "For Christ and the Church." The crisis in today's world and the changing currents in all phases of life need the positive note which our movement sounds with vigor and power. Therefore on this anniversary occasion we re-affirm our long-held conviction, "Always—for Christ and the Church."

We are convinced that young people of this day desire a full, purposeful life. There is heart-hunger for the basic values of life that will not dim or fail. There is growing certainty that Jesus Christ is the only leader who will not dis-appoint the world in its search for reality. Out of the seventy years of corporate life in holding high the banners of Christ for youth to follow, the Christian Endeavor movement enters into the new decade and next years of this century with loyalty to its principles.

Our Ecumenical Witness

This Convention rejoices in the growing sense of united witness which characterizes the Christian Church. Christian Endeavor is ecumenical in char-acter and cooperates with all Christian movements which have validity in ad-vancing causes which enrich and bless humankind. Today it accepts responsibil-ity to be in the vanguard of Christian youth groups seeking to effect a more Christian social order. It resolves to joyfully cooperate with all other groups around the world to make profound impact upon the world in the name of Christ.

This Convention by this means sends greetings to fellow Endeavorers in every land in all the world. In these last years our hearts have been saddened by the sufferings, bereavements and losses of Endeavorers in some lands. We at this gathering can only feebly understand the tragedies that envelop the lives of thousands of our youthful comrades. Yet, out of the darkest clouds come stories of glorious devotion to Christ, when loyalty to Him often means tribulation and persecution. In these testing experiences we are sure that a reborn, purified and stronger Christian church will come, led by indigenous leadership whose faith in God will make the Christian witness increasingly effective. We assure these youth that they are continually in our prayers, to the end that our Heavenly Father will sustain and strengthen them by His constant presence.

The Challenge of Communism

Whereas, atheistic communism has again demonstrated its naked aggression in Korea, with ruthless hatred of Christian principle and civilized institutions, and

Whereas, American and Canadian soldiers and other United Nations forces have been called to action to meet this aggression and have successfully met force with force, and

Whereas, the future of our Christian and democratic way of life faces a continued threat of godless aggression from without and moral corruption from within,

We are convinced, therefore, that Christian Endeavorers must daily demonstrate the strength of their personal conviction that Jesus' Sermon on the Mount offers a positive program of procedure for men and nations, and that practice of the tenets of the Christian Endeavor pledge presents the best safeguard and defense for individual members of our movement.

As we launch our Crusade for Christian Citizenship we pledge our minds and hearts to help our beloved countries make a contribution to an ordered world. We call upon the members of our movement to undergird the efforts of the United Nations to effect a just and lasting peace and to bring about reconciliation among the nations of the world in the spirit and name of Jesus Christ.

Realizing that the fellow Christians in war-torn lands and underprivileged peoples and undernourished children in distressed nations have a claim upon our purses as well as our heart-strings, we commend to all our members the support of legitimate agencies of the church and humanitarian groupings to help alleviate these tragic conditions and to aid in the rebuilding of broken bodies and communities.

Crusade For Christian Citizenship

The 41st International Convention of Christian Endeavor meets at a strategic time in the history of the nations on this continent and of the world. This is a crisis moment in the relationships of men and of nations. Thankful to Almighty God for preserving our movement and its activities for 70 years and grateful for the divinely-inspired leadership of Christian Endeavor pioneers in the realm of Christian citizenship, we affirm again at this time our belief in that form of democracy which is based on imperishable faith in God.

With consideration of this treasured heritage which grows richer with the years, and under the radiant leadership of those who reveal the resilient courage of free men and women to initiate heroic movements, we pledge to render aid in unshackling the minds of youth in other sections of the world ruthlessly hampered by unchristian philosophies. This Convention challenges Christian youth on this continent to enroll in a great crusade. This is to be a Crusade for Christian Citizenship. Herewith is sounded a clarion call to Christian youth of the great nations of the United States and Canada to assume their responsibility as Christian citizens. We would call youth to establish community life on the basis of religious faith and moral law—the only permanent foundation for freedom.

This Call to a Crusade for Christian Citizenship implies the setting up of a Department of Christian Citizenship in the International Society of Christian

Endeavor, the establishment of similar departments in state and provincial unions, the outlining of goals and objectives, of methods and techniques, the issuance of suitable literature, and the securing of funds and additional personnel that all Christian Endeavorers might attain a high level of Christian citizenship.

Meeting the Inroads of Liquor

Whereas, Throughout the seventy years of history of the movement, Christian Endeavorers have been aggressive foes of the liquor traffic and have furnished constructive leadership in the agencies that would outlaw this social evil,

We would commit ourselves again

1. To practice total abstinence,
2. To urge the passage of legislation looking toward the immediate sharp restriction and eventual elimination of liquor advertising, toward the rigid control of liquor sales, and the encouragement of communities to exercise local option.
3. To encourage in our societies, in local churches, and in public schools, education concerning the nature of alcohol as well as the individual and social effects of drinking.

The Growing Drug Menace

Whereas, we have been made newly aware of the insidious growth of the use of drugs and narcotics particularly among those of teen age, thereby enslaving youth to lifelong habits with vicious results to their body growth, mental alertness and spiritual development,

We emphatically call on Christian Endeavorers to practice complete abstinence from the use of enslaving drugs, to warn their youthful comrades regarding the same, and, to do all that is possible to expose peddlers of dope in an effort to curb this growing menace.

Resolution of Thanks

Whereas, this 41st International Convention of Christian Endeavor meeting in the hospitable city of Grand Rapids, Michigan, finds many delegates giving expression that this has been one of the best gatherings of the movement in years, and with the desire to place on permanent record our grateful recognition of all those who have contributed to this memorable Convention

We, therefore, desire to thank all those whose efforts have helped to make this gathering noteworthy in the lives of individual delegates and the host community.

Mr. Jacob H. Tigelaar and the convention Committee for untiring and thoughtful efficiency. They were delightful hosts in a fair and famous city.

Mayor Paul G. Goebel, through his representative, Mr. Porter, for his official welcome to the city.

The chief of police and his staff for courteous and kindly consideration.

Mr. Frank Whitwam, Convention Manager, and those associated with him in the Convention Bureau.

Mr. Victor C. Futrelle, Superintendent, and the Civic Auditorium staff for a constant willingness to keep the machinery running for smooth convention operation.

The officials of the Grand Rapids Chamber of Commerce and the Grand Rapids Council of Boy Scouts.

The Hotel Pantlind and all hotels of the city who so efficiently cooperated to house delegates, luncheons and group gatherings.

The ministers and churches of Grand Rapids, whose services were especially invaluable in securing homes for delegates, in sharing denominational rallies and in effecting arrangements for the orderly, worshipful and meaningful communion service.

The ushers and usherettes and page girls whose continuous help evoked continuous praise.

Dr. Clyde W. Meadows and the Program Committee for a splendid program, the product of months of careful planning, and the Field Secretaries and denominational leaders and others without whom that planning could not have been carried into the climactic results secured by the Convention.

The speakers, whose utterances have lifted delegates and visitors time and again to the very heights of vision.

Rev. Lester H. Case, the song leader, the organists and pianists and trumpeters for aiding so greatly in the ministry of song.

The Convention Choir, Dr. Henry A. Bruinsma, director, for adding to the beauty and spiritual power of the evening services.

The newspapers of Grand Rapids, the Associated Press, the United Press, and the papers of the country for their continued presentation of convention news, and to Miss Lois Ludowic for her direction of the publicity for the Convention.

The broadcasting stations for generous donation of time for broadcasts to the community and countryside.

The leaders of local societies, county and Michigan State Unions whose loyalty and cooperation were invaluable.

The staff officers, Dr. Gene Stone and Rev. Charles E. F. Howe who, together with their office aides, carried the burden of administration, perhaps beyond all others, yet never lost amidst their responsibilities that friendly, kindly touch which has endeared them to Christian Endeavor.

To all who have in any way enabled this great throng of young people to enjoy an unforgettable week, in a friendly city, we extend our genuine thanks.

> Raymond M. Veh, chairman
> Harold Dudley
> Harold E. Westerhoff

Convention Hall Sidelights

Dr. Daniel A. Poling, who is president of the World's Union of Christian Endeavor, and presently candidate for mayor of Philadelphia, Pa., made three trips back and forth between Grand Rapids and his city during Convention week to keep in touch with campaign developments there and the Christian Endeavor Convention program in Grand Rapids.

* * * *

Joseph Holton Jones, architect of Wilmington, Delaware, flew to Grand Rapids Wednesday, flying back on Thursday, just to be present at the Christian Endeavor banquet Wednesday evening to see his wife receive International Youth's Distinguished Service citation.

* * * *

Lois Ludowic, chief of the reportorial staff, encouraged good comradeship in the press room by supplying daily refreshments to officials who wandered into the press room as well as to the usherettes and Boy Scouts. She gave the trustees a real thrill when she said, "I believe everyone should go after new *Christian Endeavor World* subscriptions. I am sending out subscriptions to my friends so that they will be able to keep in touch with our growing movement."

* * * *

Forty Christian Endeavorers left the Convention Sunday evening for an extended tour of the Pacific Coast under the leadership of Charles E. F. Howe, Associate Secretary and Treasurer of the Christian Endeavor movement. The tour group visited Canadian national parks, Yosemite and Sequoia Parks, Los Angeles, and Grand Canyon in a three-weeks swing about the western section of the nation.

* * * *

Over forty of the participants to the World's Convention of Christian Endeavor held in July, 1950 in London, England, were in attendance at the Grand Rapids gathering. These delegates one night met to revive memories by seeing slides taken by selected members of the tour party.

* * * *

A big policeman expressed his displeasure on Thursday night at the change of the evening session from the Speedrome to the Civic Auditorium. "I just don't like it. I just don't like it," he was heard to repeat. When somebody asked him what he didn't like, he said, "This change of the big rally from Comstock Park to inside. If this rally had been held at the park, I was to have been there and could have heard Billy Graham's message. Now I have got to stay outside on the street to direct traffic."

* * * *

Hotels and churches across the city were meeting places for various denominational and state delegation dinners. "Did you ever taste better food than found in Grand Rapids?" many delegates asked.

At the Convention banquet Wednesday evening 130 churchmen and women of this city put on aprons and rolled up their sleeves to serve the meal and later wash dishes. The banquet was served in record time. As with few banquets served anywhere today, there were "seconds" and even "thirds" for the 1,014 in the lower convention hall.

* * * *

The coffee shop waitresses as well as the drug store clerks appreciated the spirit and kindliness of the delegates. The comment everywhere was about the fine spirit of the group which this convention brought to the city.

* * * *

From Wednesday night on, Mrs. Joseph Holton Jones was constantly addressed as Mrs. Christian Endeavor. With the passing of Father and Mother Clark, beloved founders of the movement, friends of Christian Endeavor felt that they have another tie with the past in Mrs. Jones being named as "Mrs. Christian Endeavor."

* * * *

Newspaper and radio coverage of the Convention was admirable. The advance publicity, planned by Grand Rapids Christian Endeavorers was unusual. From early morning through the noon-time "minute of Prayer", through the broadcasting of major parts of evening services the Convention was heard over the local stations and nation-wide hook-ups by a vast number of people.

* * * *

We'll See You

at the

Forty-Second Convention
of the
The International Society of
Christian Endeavor

DENVER, COLORADO
June 22-28, 1953

The seven young people who as representatives of their local church youth groups were guests of THE LOOKOUT at the convention are shown with Editor Guy P. Leavitt of LOOKOUT magazine, Mrs. Leavitt and Dr. Bryan. Left to right are Dr. Bryan; Joan Benson, Crusaders Christian Youth Fellowship, Lincoln Avenue Christian Church, Youngstown, O.; John McMillan, representative of the C. E. Society, First Christian Church, Lake Wales, Fla.; Joan Lytle, representative of the C. Y. F. of the Lincoln Avenue Church, Youngstown, O.; Bob Sanders, representative, C. E. Society, Church of Christ, Beaverton, Ore.; Ellen Clampitt, representative, Young People's Society, Zoah Christian Church, near Scottsburg, Ind.; Sam Kingsbury, representative, Senior C. E. Society, First Christian Church, Fort Pierce, Fla.; Mrs. Guy P. Leavitt; Darrell Low and Darlene Ann Maltsberger, both representing the Christian Youth Fellowship, First Christian Church, Pryor, Okla.; and Duane Merritt, Fort Pierce, Fla.

Grand Rapids Civic Auditorium

The Ohio delegation won first place in advance registrations.

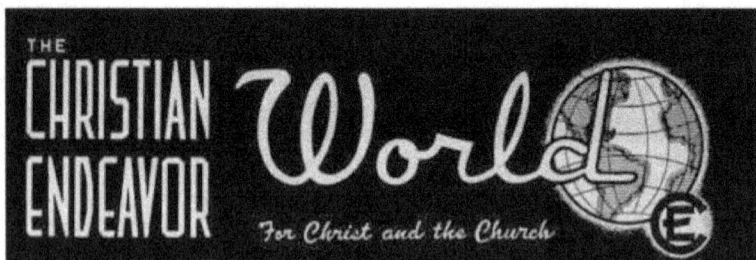

Choir and Participants in Thursday Evening Service.

www.ingramcontent.com/pod-product-compliance
Lightning Source LLC
Chambersburg PA
CBHW020519030426
42337CB00011B/464